The WI Book of
BISCUITS

Published by WI Books Ltd
in associatiation with
Southgate Publishers Ltd
Glebe House, Church Street,
Crediton, Devon EX17 2AF

First impression 1983

Reprinted 1992

The WI book of biscuits
  1. Cookies
  641.8'654 TX772

ISBN 0-900556-76-5

Printed in Great Britain by Short Run Press Ltd,
Exeter

ACKNOWLEDGEMENTS
WI Books Ltd is grateful to the
Cumbria-Westmorland Federation
of Women's Institutions for their
kind permission to reproduce
recipes previously published in
Biscuits Galore.
  We would also like to thank
Sally Lister and Pat Hesketh for
their advice and contributions.
  We wish to acknowledge the
Cumbria-Cumberland Federation
of Women's Institutes for allowing
us to reproduce some of the recipes
in their publication *Crisp and
Crunchy*.

The WI Book of Biscuits

Contents

Helpful Hints 6

Sweet Biscuits
Abbey Biscuits 8
Almond Balls
Almond Butter Crisps 9
Almond Cocoroons
Alphabet Biscuits 10
Anzac Cookies
Appleby Fairings 11
Apricot Shortcakes
Auntie Dot's Cookies 12
Basic Drop Cookies 13
Belgian Sugar Biscuits 14
Blantyre Biscuits
Bourbon Biscuits 15
Bufton Biscuits 16
Burnt Butter Biscuits 17
Butter Cookies
Buttercrunch 18
Caramel Biscuits 19
Caraway Biscuits 20
Cardamom Cookies
Catherine Wheels 21
Cherry and Chocolate Chews 22
Cherry Snowballs
Cherry Whirls 23
Chestnut Biscuits
Chocolate Biscuits 24
Chocolate Cherry Biscuits
Chocolate Chip Biscuits 25
Chocolate Nut Biscuits
Chocolate Oat Biscuits 26
Chocolate Peppermint Creams 27
Chocolate Stars 28
Chocolate Wagon Wheels
Cinnamon Bars 29

Coconut Biscuits
Coconut Butter Biscuits 30
Coconut and Cherry Slices
Coconut Crisps 31
Coconut Drops
Coconut Kisses 32
Coffee Kisses
Coffee Walnut Biscuits 33
Cornish Ginger Fairings
Coupland Biscuits 34
Crescent Biscuits
Crisps 35
Creston Drops
Crunchies 36
Crunchy Biscuits
Cumberland Snaps 37
Curly Peters
Danish Specier Biscuits 38
Date Slices
Date Sticks 39
Dream Cookies
Drop Cookies 40
Easter Biscuits 41
Easter Bunny Biscuits 42
Finnish Shortbread 43
Firelighter Biscuits
Flaked Almond Biscuits 44
Florentines
Freezer Biscuits 45
Fruity Brittles 46
Fruity Snaps
Garibaldi Biscuits 47
German Almond Biscuits 48
German Biscuits
Ginger Biscuits 49
Ginger Ruffles 50
Ginger Snaps

Gipsy Creams 51
Gipsy Crisps 52
Grantham Ginger Drops
Grasmere Gingerbread 53
Ground Rice Cookies
Highlanders 54
Honey Biscuits
Iced Ginger Shortcake 55
Iced Peppermint Biscuits 56
Iced Raspberry Biscuits 57
Joyce's Biscuits 58
Jumbles
Kelvin Crisps 59
King Haakon Biscuits 60
Kourabiédes
Kringles 61
Lace Biscuits 62
Lancashire Nuts
Lemon Crescents 63
Lemon Fudge Biscuits 64
Macaroons 65
Ma' Moule
Marzipan Biscuits 66
Melting Moments 67
Napoleon Biscuits 68
Napoleon Hats 69
Novelty Biscuits 70
Nut and Fruit Shortbread
Oat Biscuits 71
Oatmeal Biscuits
Orange Coconut Crisps 72
Peanut Butter Cookies 73
Peanut Cookies
Peppermint Oat Biscuits 74
Petits Fours 75
Raisin Shortcake 76
Rice Biscuits
Rich Biscuits 77
Rolled Oat Biscuits
Semolina Pyramid Biscuits 78
Shortbread Biscuits
Shrewsbury Biscuits 79
Strawberry Delights
Tebay Crunch 80
Tuilles

Vanilla Kipferl 81
Viennese Biscuits 82
Walnut Bars 83
Walnut Crisps
Wheaten Biscuits 84
Wholemeal Shortcake
Yo-Yo's 85

Savoury Biscuits
Bacon and Oatmeal Biscuits 87
Celery Biscuits
Cheese Biscuits 88
Cheese Crackers
Cheese Sablés 89
Cheese Straws
Crackamacs 90
Curry Knots
Digestive Biscuits 91
Guernsey Biscuits
Oatcakes 92
Paprika Cheese Biscuits
Walnut Savoury Biscuits 93
Wholemeal Savoury Titbits

What is the WI? 94

Index 95

5

Helpful Hints

1. Measure all the ingredients carefully. Always use level spoonfuls where spoon measurements are given unless the recipe specifies otherwise.

2. Do not switch from metric to imperial units part-way through a recipe. Work consistently in either one unit of measurement or the other.

3. Use a soft flour wherever possible. Ordinary flour can be made softer by substituting one tablespoon of cornflour for one tablespoon in eight ounces of flour. Sieve them together.

4. In all the recipes, wholemeal flour and brown sugar can be used instead of white flour and white sugar, if preferred.

5. Make sure that all the ingredients are well mixed.

6. If you are using the melting method, do not overheat the syrup as this will result in a toffee mixture. A gentle heat is sufficient to melt the fat and the syrup.

7. To ensure that the biscuits keep their shape and do not join together, space them well apart on the baking tray. Unless the recipe specifies an ungreased tray, this should be well-greased to prevent the biscuits from sticking.

8. A moderate oven temperature is usually preferable as biscuits are thin and too hot an oven will cause them to burn. Most biscuits will darken very little in colour while baking.

9. When they are fully baked, allow the biscuits to cool for a few minutes on the baking sheet before moving them to a cooling tray — this ensures crispness.

10. Once they are completely cold, store the biscuits immediately in an airtight container. Use separate containers for cakes and biscuits: when the two are stored together, biscuits lose their crispness.

11. If the biscuits are to be sandwiched together with a filling, do this just before serving them to avoid loss of crispness.

Sweet Biscuits

A

Abbey Biscuits

INGREDIENTS
150g (5 oz) plain flour
150g (5 oz) margarine
150g (5 oz) caster sugar
125g (4 oz) rolled oats
1 tbsp milk
1 tsp golden syrup
1 tsp bicarbonate of soda

METHOD
Cream the margarine and sugar
together, then add the milk,
bicarbonate of soda and syrup. Stir
in the flour and oats and mix well.
Roll the dough into small balls and
space them evenly apart on a
baking tray. Bake them for 25
minutes until they are golden
brown.
Oven 150°C/300°F. Gas 2.

Almond Balls

INGREDIENTS
100g (4 oz) plain flour
100g (4 oz) butter or margarine
100g (4 oz) caster sugar
100g (4 oz) ground almonds
1 egg
1 tsp vanilla essence
slivers of almonds

METHOD
Cream the butter and sugar
together. Stir in the ground
almonds, the yolk of the egg, the
vanilla essence and the flour.
Knead the dough until it is well
blended.
    Roll it into small balls about
2.5cm (1 in) in diameter. Press a
slivered almond on top of each one
and brush them with the slightly
beaten white of the egg. Bake them
in a moderately slow oven for 10 to
12 minutes.
    The butter and almonds will
keep these biscuits fresh for several
weeks.
Oven 170°C/335°F. Gas 3-4.

Almond Butter Crisps

INGREDIENTS
225g (8 oz) self-raising flour
200g (7 oz) butter or margarine
175g (6 oz) caster sugar
1 tsp vanilla essence
1 tsp bicarbonate of soda
split almonds

METHOD
Work the butter into the sugar and when this has been absorbed, add the vanilla essence. Sieve the bicarbonate with the flour and add them to the other ingredients. Knead the dough together.

Roll it into balls the size of a walnut and arrange them on oiled trays leaving room for the biscuits to flatten and spread. Top each one with a split almond. Bake them in a moderate oven for 15 minutes or until they are golden brown.

These light-as-air biscuits are often served in Denmark. This recipe makes 48 biscuits.
Oven 180°C/350°F. Gas 4.

Almond Cocoroons

INGREDIENTS
100g (4 oz) caster sugar
75g (3 oz) desiccated coconut
35g (1½ oz) ground almonds
2 egg whites
rice paper

METHOD
Whisk the egg whites. Mix the coconut, ground almonds and sugar together and fold them lightly into the beaten egg.

Place the mixture in small rounds (about 2 tsp at a time) on rice paper. This recipe makes about 24 biscuits. Bake them for 20 to 25 minutes.
Oven 160°C/325°F. Gas 3.

Alphabet Biscuits

INGREDIENTS
Biscuits:
225g (8 oz) plain flour
150g (5 oz) butter
50g (2 oz) caster sugar
¼ tsp cinnamon
pinch of salt
1 tbsp water
caster sugar to glaze

Icing:
100g (4 oz) icing sugar
1 tbsp water

METHOD
For the biscuits, rub the butter into the dry ingredients to the consistency of fine breadcrumbs. Stir in the sugar and water and knead the dough.

Roll it out thinly and cut it into small squares. Brush them with water and sprinkle them with caster sugar to glaze. Bake them for 15 to 20 minutes then allow them to cool.

For the icing, mix the sieved icing sugar with the water and beat them to a smooth consistency. Pipe letters onto each biscuit.
Oven 180°C/350° F. Gas 4.

Anzac (Australian) Cookies

INGREDIENTS
175g (6 oz) butter
175g (6 oz) caster sugar
125g (4 oz) plain flour
125g (4 oz) raisins
125g (4 oz) rolled oats
1 tsp golden syrup
1 tsp bicarbonate of soda
2 tbsp boiling water

METHOD
Melt the butter and the syrup. Dissolve the bicarbonate of soda in the water and add this to the butter. Mix together the flour, oats, sugar and the chopped raisins and pour in the liquid. Mix them well.

Place the dough in teaspoonfuls on greased trays, allowing room for spreading. Bake them for about 15 minutes. Remove the biscuits from the trays and allow them to cool.
Oven 150°C/300°F. Gas 2.

Appleby Fairings

(Traditional recipe for Whit Monday Hirings)

INGREDIENTS
450g (1 lb) plain flour
275g (10 oz) butter
225g (8 oz) caster sugar
1 egg yolk
pinch of salt

METHOD
Rub the butter into the flour, then add the sugar and salt. Drop in the egg yolk. Work the mixture into a dry dough.

Roll it out to 0.5cm (¼ in) thick and cut it into rounds. Impress the biscuits with a pattern or prick them all over. Bake them for about 35 to 40 minutes.
Oven 180-190°C/350-375°F. Gas 4-5.

Apricot Shortcakes

INGREDIENTS
175g (6 oz) plain flour
125g (4 oz) butter
50g (2 oz) ground rice
50g (2 oz) caster sugar
35g (1½ oz) apricot jam
caster sugar for dredging
extra jam for decoration

METHOD
Rub the butter into the flour. Add the ground rice and sugar and mix them together. Put the jam in the centre of the mixture and work it into a smooth paste.

Roll it out to about 2cm (¾ in) thick. Cut it into fancy shapes. Make a small hollow in the centre of each biscuit with a thimble and put a little jam in the hole. Bake them in a moderate oven for about 20 minutes. Leave them to cool then dredge them with caster sugar.
Oven 180-190°C/350-375°F. Gas 4-5.

Auntie Dot's Cookies

INGREDIENTS
75g (3 oz) self-raising flour
75g (3 oz) caster sugar
75g (3 oz) butter or margarine
75g (3 oz) raisins
a little egg
cornflakes

METHOD
Cream the fat and sugar. Stir in
the flour and about half a beaten
egg to make a very stiff dough.
Then add the raisins.

Roll teaspoons of the mixture
into balls, then roll them in
cornflakes. Place them on greased
baking trays, leaving plenty of
room for them to spread. Bake for
about 12 minutes. This recipe
makes 18 biscuits.
Oven 180°C/350°F. Gas 4.

B

Basic Drop Cookies

INGREDIENTS
225g (8 oz) plain flour
75g (3 oz) caster sugar
75g (3 oz) margarine
1 egg
½ tsp baking powder
½ tsp) vanilla essence
3 tbsp milk

METHOD
Cream the fat and sugar, then add the beaten egg. Sieve the flour and baking powder together. Add them to the creamed mixture alternately with the milk and vanilla essence. Not all the milk may be needed as the mixture must not be too soft.

Drop teaspoonfuls of the mixture onto a greased tray, leaving room for the biscuits to spread. Bake them for 10 to 16 minutes.
Oven 180°C/350°F. Gas 4.

VARIATIONS
Substitute soft brown sugar to make a light brown cookie.
Fruit and Nut Cookie: add 75g (3 oz) dried fruit and 25g (1 oz) chopped nuts.
Cinnamon Wafer: add 1 tsp powdered cinnamon to the dry mixture.
Chocolate Wafer: substitute 1 tbsp cocoa for 25g (1 oz) flour.

All the cookies may be iced and decorated in many ways.

13

Belgian Sugar Biscuits

INGREDIENTS
175g (6 oz) plain flour
150g (5 oz) caster sugar
75g (3 oz) butter
1 tsp ground ginger
1 egg yolk

METHOD
Cream the butter and sugar, then add the egg yolk. Add the sifted flour and ginger, and mix thoroughly. Shape the dough into a 6-7cm (2-2½ in) roll and leave it in the fridge or a cool place for a day.

Using a sharp knife, cut the roll into thin slices of approximately 0.5cm (¼ in). Bake them on a greased tray until the biscuits are lightly browned (about 15 to 20 minutes).
Oven 160°C/325°F. Gas 3.

Blantyre Biscuits

INGREDIENTS
100g (4 oz) rolled oats
100g (4 oz) caster sugar
100g (4 oz) wholemeal flour
100g (4 oz) butter or margarine
2 bananas or 75g (3 oz) chopped nuts
1 egg
½ tsp baking powder

METHOD
Beat together the sugar and butter. Mix in the oats, flour and baking powder. Add the egg and divide the dough into two portions.

Put one half into a greased shallow tin and press it down with a fork. Spread the sliced bananas or nuts over this and cover them with the remaining dough. Press it down. Bake it in a moderate oven for 15 to 20 minutes or until it is golden brown. Cut it into fingers.
Oven 180°C/350°F. Gas 4.

Bourbon Biscuits

together. When the biscuits are cool, sandwich them together with the filling.
Oven 160°C/325°F. Gas 3.

INGREDIENTS
Biscuits:
100g (4 oz) plain flour
50g (2 oz) butter
50g (2 oz) caster sugar
1 tbsp golden syrup
15g (½ oz) cocoa
½ tsp baking powder
granulated sugar

Filling:
50g (2 oz) icing sugar
25g (1 oz) plain chocolate
1½ tbsp water
vanilla essence to taste

METHOD
To make the biscuits, sift together the dry ingredients. Cream the butter and caster sugar until they are light and fluffy. Beat in the syrup and stir in half of the flour mixture. Turn the dough out on to a working-surface and knead in the remaining flour mixture.

Roll it out to a thickness of 0.5cm (¼ in), sprinkle it with granulated sugar and press it with a rolling pin. Cut it into neat fingers and place them on a greased baking tray. Bake them for 15 to 20 minutes.

For the filling, melt the chocolate in the water, add the icing sugar, and beat them

Bufton Biscuits

cream them together. Add the cocoa powder and coffee essence and beat the mixture well. Oven 180°C/350°F. Gas 4.

INGREDIENTS
Biscuits:
150g (5 oz) margarine
100g (4 oz) self-raising flour
100g (4 oz) granulated sugar
100g (4 oz) rolled oats
2 tbsp golden syrup
2 tsp milk
25g (1 oz) semolina
1 tsp baking powder
1 tsp bicarbonate of soda
pinch of salt

Filling:
100g (4 oz) icing sugar
50g (2 oz) butter
1 tsp cocoa powder
1 tsp coffee essence

METHOD
For the biscuits, cream the margarine and sugar. Add the flour, semolina, oats, syrup, salt and baking powder. Lastly, add the bicarbonate of soda mixed with the milk.

Make small, rough balls and cook them on a greased tray for 15-20 minutes until they are set.

When the biscuits are cool, serve them plain or sandwich them together with mocha butter cream.

To make the filling, cream the butter until it is soft. Gradually add the sieved icing sugar and

Burnt Butter Biscuits

INGREDIENTS
175g (6 oz) self-raising flour
125g (4 oz) butter
125g (4 oz) caster sugar
1 egg

METHOD
Put the butter in a saucepan and cook it until it is golden brown. Pour it into a bowl and leave it to cool. When it is set, mix in the sugar and beat well. Add the egg and flour and mix them to a stiff consistency.

Roll the dough into small balls and bake them for about 15 minutes.
Oven 180°C/350°F. Gas 4.

Butter Cookies

INGREDIENTS
225g (8 oz) plain flour
175g (6 oz) butter
100g (4 oz) soft brown sugar
25g (1 oz) demerara sugar

METHOD
Cream the butter and the soft brown sugar until they are light in colour. Blend in the flour and work the mixture to a smooth dough. Divide it into two sausages, then roll them in the demerara sugar. Leave them to cool in the fridge until they are stiff.

Cut them into slices and place them on greased trays. Bake them for 20 minutes.
Oven 180°C/350°F. Gas 4.

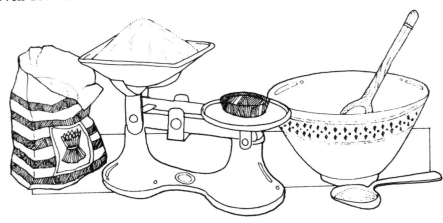

Buttercrunch

INGREDIENTS
225g (8 oz) self-raising flour
175g (6 oz) butter
175g (6 oz) demerara sugar
125g (4 oz) rolled oats
2 tbsp golden syrup
pinch of salt

METHOD
Rub the butter into the dry
ingredients and mix in the syrup to
make a firm dough. Break off
pieces the size of a walnut and roll
them in your hands.
    Place them on a greased baking
sheet and flatten them slightly.
Bake them for 15 to 20 minutes.
Oven 180° C/350°F. Gas 4.

C

Caramel Biscuits

minutes, stirring all the time. When it is cool, pour it over the base and leave it to set.

For the topping, melt the chocolate and pour it over the caramel. When it is quite set, cut it into fingers.

Oven 180°C/350°F. Gas 4.

INGREDIENTS
Base:
175g (6 oz) self-raising flour
125g (4 oz) butter
50g (2 oz) caster sugar

Caramel:
200g (7 oz) tin of condensed milk
125g (4 oz) margarine
50g (2 oz) caster sugar
2 tbsp golden syrup
few drops of vanilla essence

Topping:
200g (7 oz) chocolate

METHOD
For the base, cream the butter and sugar, then mix in the flour. Press the dough into a 30 x 20cm (12 x 8 in) baking tin and bake it for 15 minutes until it is golden brown. Leave it to cool.

For the caramel, put all the ingredients in a pan and melt them over a gentle heat. Bring it to the boil. Boil the mixture for 5

Caraway Biscuits

Cardamom Cookies

Caraway Biscuits

INGREDIENTS
175g (6 oz) self-raising flour
125g (4 oz) margarine
50g (2 oz) icing sugar
1 tsp caraway seeds
a little milk

METHOD
Cream the margarine and icing sugar, then add the flour and caraway seeds. Mix them to a stiff paste with a little milk. Roll the dough out to a thickness of 0.5cm (¼ in) and cut it into shapes. Bake them for 15 minutes or until they are golden brown.
Oven 180°C/350°F. Gas 4.

Cardamom Cookies

INGREDIENTS
225g (8 oz) softened butter
225g (8 oz) plain flour
75g (3 oz) icing sugar
50g (2 oz) chopped walnuts
1 tsp almond essence
½ tsp ground cardamom
pinch of salt
icing sugar to dredge

METHOD
Sift the icing sugar. Add the rest of the ingredients and blend to a firm mixture. Shape the dough into 2.5cm (1 in) balls and place them, spaced 5cm (2 in) apart on greased baking trays. Bake for 20 minutes or until they are golden brown. Dredge the cookies with icing sugar before serving. This recipe makes 30 biscuits.
Oven 180°C/350°F. Gas 4.

Catherine Wheels

they are golden brown. Leave them to cool on a wire rack before dredging them with the remaining caster sugar.
Oven 160°C/325°F. Gas 3.

INGREDIENTS
175g (6 oz) plain flour
100g (4 oz) caster sugar
75g (3 oz) butter
½ egg
1 tsp milk
½ tsp baking powder
1 tbsp cocoa powder
½ tsp vanilla essence
pinch of salt

METHOD
Cream the butter and 75g (3 oz) of the sugar. Gradually beat in the egg. Sift together the flour with the baking powder and salt. Fold them into the creamed mixture to make a soft dough. Divide the dough into two equal parts. Add the sifted cocoa and milk to one portion. Work it gently with your fingertips. Add the essence to the other portion.

Roll each piece into a 25 x 15cm (10 x 6 in) oblong. Place the cocoa dough on top of the essence dough. Roll the two layers up closely and firmly from one long side. Wrap the roll in foil and chill it in the fridge for 30 minutes.

Grease two baking sheets. Cut the dough into 24 slices. Place them on the baking sheets and bake in the centre of a pre-heated oven for 15 to 20 minutes or until

Cherry and Chocolate Chews

INGREDIENTS
175g (6 oz) self-raising flour
125g (4 oz) butter
75g (3 oz) plain cooking chocolate
50g (2 oz) caster sugar
50g (2 oz) glacé cherries
2 tbsp condensed milk
pinch of salt

METHOD
Cream the butter and sugar, then beat in the milk. Sift in the flour and salt. Chop the chocolate and cherries into small pieces. Mix all the ingredients well together.

Take good teaspoonfuls of the mixture and form them into balls. Place them on a greased baking sheet and flatten them slightly. Bake them for about 25 minutes. This recipe makes 35 biscuits. Oven 180°C/350°F. Gas 4.

Cherry Snowballs

INGREDIENTS
225g (8 oz) plain flour
225g (8 oz) butter
50g (2 oz) icing sugar
100g (4 oz) chopped walnuts
1 tsp vanilla essence
pinch of salt
glacé cherries
fine sugar for rolling

METHOD
Cream the butter with the icing sugar until they are fluffy. Add the rest of the ingredients except for the cherries and mix them well.

Flatten teaspoonfuls of the dough in the palms of your hands. Place a cherry on each circle and cover it by pinching the dough up round it. Roll them into balls and place on a greased baking sheet. Bake them for 35 minutes. While they are still hot, roll the biscuits in fine sugar. This recipe makes 36 biscuits. Oven 160°C/325°F. Gas 3.

Cherry Whirls

Chestnut Biscuits

INGREDIENTS
175g (6 oz) plain flour
175g (6 oz) butter
50g (2 oz) icing sugar
1 tsp vanilla essence
8 or 9 glacé cherries

METHOD
Cream the butter until it is light and soft. Add the icing sugar and vanilla essence. Stir in the flour.

Transfer the mixture to a large piping bag fitted with a star-shaped nozzle. Pipe 16 to 18 fairly small whirls onto two greased baking trays. Top each one with half a cherry. Bake them in the centre of the oven for 20 minutes, or until they are pale gold.

Leave them on the trays for 5 minutes before transferring them to a cooling rack. Store them in an airtight tin when they are cold.
Oven 160°C/325°F. Gas 3.

INGREDIENTS
225g (8 oz) plain flour
125g (4 oz) butter
125g (4 oz) caster sugar
1 egg yolk
1 tsp chestnut purée

METHOD
Cream the butter and sugar. Add the egg yolk and flour and lastly the purée. Knead them together.

Roll out the dough and cut it into rounds. Place them on greased trays and bake them in a slow oven for 30 minutes or until they are golden brown.
Oven 150-160°C/300-325°F. Gas 2-3.

Chocolate Biscuits

INGREDIENTS
Biscuits:
175g (6 oz) self-raising flour
175g (6 oz) caster sugar
75g (3 oz) butter
1 tbsp cocoa powder
1 egg
1 tsp vanilla essence

Topping:
chocolate

METHOD
Cream the butter and sugar until they are light and creamy. Add the egg and vanilla essence and beat again. Mix in the sifted flour and cocoa.

Roll teaspoonfuls of the dough into balls, place them on a greased baking sheet and flatten them slightly. Bake them for about 15 minutes.

When the biscuits are cold, ice them with melted chocolate. This recipe makes 24 biscuits.
Oven 190°C/375°F. Gas 5.

Chocolate Cherry Biscuits

INGREDIENTS
100g (4 oz) softened butter
100g (4 oz) plain flour
50g (2 oz) caster sugar
25g (1 oz) glacé cherries
25g (1 oz) plain chocolate
½ tsp vanilla essence

METHOD
Cream the butter and sugar and add the vanilla essence. Chop the cherries and the chocolate finely and add them to the mixture. Stir in the flour.

Place 18 to 20 teaspoonfuls of the mixture on a well greased baking tray, leaving space for the biscuits to spread. Bake for 15 to 20 minutes.
Oven 190°C/375°F. Gas 5.

Chocolate Chip Biscuits

INGREDIENTS
175g (6 oz) self-raising flour
100g (4 oz) butter
100g (4 oz) caster sugar
75g (3 oz) plain chocolate
2 tbsp condensed milk

METHOD
Cream the butter and sugar together until they are soft, then cream in the condensed milk. Break the chocolate into chips the size of sultanas and add them to the creamed ingredients. Sieve the flour into the mixture. Mix the dough well then roll it into walnut-sized balls. Place them on a greased tray and press them down with a fork. Bake them for 25-30 minutes or until they are golden brown.
Oven 150°C/300°F Gas 2.

Chocolate Nut Biscuits

INGREDIENTS
225g (8 oz) plain flour
175g (6 oz) caster sugar
125g (4 oz) butter
35g (1½ oz) chopped walnuts
35g (1½ oz) chocolate
1 egg
½ tsp cream of tartar
½ tsp bicarbonate of soda
few drops of vanilla essence
pinch of salt

METHOD
Cream the butter. Add the sugar and cream them together. Add the egg, then add the grated chocolate together with all the other ingredients. Form the dough into a roll about 4cm (1½ in) in diameter and place it in the fridge.
When it is thoroughly chilled, slice it with a sharp knife. Bake the biscuits on a greased tin for 10 minutes.
Oven 180°C/350°F. Gas 4.

Chocolate Oat Biscuits

For the filling, cream the butter until it is soft. Add the sieved icing sugar and cream them together. Add the vanilla essence and beat the mixture well.

Sandwich the biscuits together in pairs with the filling and coat the tops with melted chocolate.

Oven 180°/350°F. Gas 4.

INGREDIENTS

Biscuits:
100g (4 oz) self-raising flour
100g (4 oz) rolled oats
75g (3 oz) caster sugar
50g (2 oz) lard
50g (2 oz) margarine
1 tsp golden syrup
1 tsp bicarbonate of soda
1 tsp vanilla essence
1 tbsp boiling water

Filling:
100g (4 oz) icing sugar
50g (2 oz) butter
1 tbsp cocoa powder

Topping:
cooking chocolate

METHOD

For the biscuits, rub the lard and margarine into the mixed flour, oats and sugar. Mix the remaining ingredients together and add them to make a fairly soft mixture. Knead the dough into a ball and put it in the fridge for 30 minutes.

Roll it out and cut it into rounds. Cook the biscuits in a moderate oven for about 20 minutes and leave them to cool.

Chocolate Peppermint Creams

the melted cooking chocolate and cut the biscuit into pieces when the chocolate has set.
Oven 190°C/375°F. Gas 5.

INGREDIENTS
Base:
100g (4 oz) butter
100g (4 oz) plain flour
75g (3 oz) desiccated coconut
50g (2 oz) caster sugar
1 tbsp drinking chocolate
½ tsp baking powder

Filling:
75g (3 oz) icing sugar
75g (3 oz) butter
¼ tsp peppermint essence
drop of green food colouring

Topping:
100g (4 oz) cooking chocolate

METHOD
For the base, cream the butter and sugar, then add the baking powder, drinking chocolate, flour and coconut. Press the mixture into a Swiss roll tin. Bake it for about 15 to 20 minutes on the middle shelf of the oven until it is an even colour all over. Leave it to cool.

For the filling, cream the butter and sugar, then add the essence and colouring. Spread it over the base.

Cover the layer of filling with

Chocolate Stars

INGREDIENTS
225g (8 oz) plain flour
125g (4 oz) butter
125g (4 oz) caster sugar
50g (2 oz) chocolate drops
25g (1 oz) cornflour
15g (½ oz) cocoa powder
1 egg
2 tsp milk
½ tsp vanilla essence
pinch of salt

METHOD
Sieve the flour, cornflour, cocoa and salt into a bowl. Cream the butter and sugar until they are light and fluffy. Beat in the egg and vanilla essence. Work in the flour mixture and mix it to a soft dough with the milk.

Put the mixture into a large forcing bag fitted with a large star nozzle. Pipe stars 4cm (1½ in) in diameter, and spaced well apart, on greased baking sheets. Place a chocolate drop in the centre of each star. Bake them in the centre of the oven for 15 minutes. Cool them on a wire rack.
Oven 160°C/325°F. Gas 3.

Chocolate Wagon Wheels

INGREDIENTS
100g (4 oz) plain flour
50g (2 oz) margarine
25g (1 oz) caster sugar
25g (1 oz) chocolate
few drops vanilla essence
pinch of salt
a little egg

METHOD
Sieve the flour and salt and rub in the margarine. Add the sugar and essence and mix them to a dough with the beaten egg.

Roll it out on a lightly-floured board and cut out 5cm (2 in) rounds with a plain cutter. Bake them on a greased baking tray in a hot oven for about 10 minutes.

When the biscuits are cold, melt the chocolate over hot water. Dip each biscuit half-way into the chocolate and smooth its surface with a knife. Leave them to set on a wire tray.
Oven 200°C/400°F. Gas 6.

Cinnamon Bars

Coconut Biscuits

INGREDIENTS
150g (5 oz) plain flour
100g (4 oz) margarine
75g (3 oz) caster sugar
2 tsp ground cinnamon
½ egg
pinch of salt
chopped nuts

METHOD
Cream the margarine and sugar
until they are white and fluffy.
Beat in the egg, reserving a little of
the white for glazing. Gradually
add the dry ingredients to the
creamed mixture.
Press the dough into an oblong
tin. Brush the surface with egg
white and sprinkle it with chopped
nuts. Bake it in a very slow oven
for 1 hour. Cut it into slices and
allow them to cool.
Oven 140°C/275°F. Gas 1.

INGREDIENTS
75g (3 oz) plain flour
75g (3 oz) caster sugar
50g (2 oz) butter
25g (1 oz) desiccated coconut
1 egg

METHOD
Cream the butter and sugar
together until light in colour. Beat
in the egg. Fold in the flour and
the coconut. Put teaspoons of the
mixture on trays and bake them for
about 10 to 15 minutes.
Oven 160°C/325°. Gas 3.

Coconut Butter Biscuits

Coconut and Cherry Slices

INGREDIENTS
225g (8 oz) self-raising flour
175g (6 oz) butter or margarine
175g (6 oz) caster sugar
125g (4 oz) desiccated coconut
2 tbsp golden syrup
½ tsp bicarbonate of soda

INGREDIENTS
150g (5 oz) cooking chocolate
100g (4 oz) caster sugar
100g (4 oz) desiccated coconut
50g (2 oz) margarine
1 egg
50g (2 oz) glacé cherries

METHOD
Melt the butter and syrup in a pan and add the coconut. Sieve the flour and bicarbonate of soda into the mixture and stir it well. Lastly, stir in the sugar.

Shape the dough into small balls, and place them on greased trays leaving room for the biscuits to spread. Bake them for 12 to 15 minutes.
Oven 180°C/350°F. Gas 4.

METHOD
Line a Swiss roll tin with foil. Melt the chocolate. Spread it over the foil and leave it to cool.

Cream the margarine and sugar. Beat in with the egg. Chop the cherries and mix in with the coconut. Spread this mixture over the cooled chocolate. Cook for 15 to 20 minutes. When the biscuit is cool, cut it into slices. Store them in an airtight tin.
Oven 170°C/335°F. Gas 3-4.

Coconut Crisps

INGREDIENTS
225g (8 oz) self-raising flour
225g (8 oz) soft margarine
75g (3 oz) icing sugar
25g (1 oz) desiccated coconut
drop of vanilla essence

METHOD
Cream all the ingredients except for the coconut. Form the mixture into small balls and roll them in the coconut. Place them on greased trays and bake them for about 20 minutes until they are golden brown.
Oven 160°C/325°. Gas 3.

Coconut Drops

INGREDIENTS
225g (8 oz) desiccated coconut
125g (4 oz) granulated sugar
2 egg whites

METHOD
Beat the egg white until it is stiff. Add the sugar and coconut and beat them all together.
Drop small teaspoonfuls of the mixture onto greased paper and bake them in a moderate oven for about 20 minutes.
Oven 180°C/350°F. Gas 4.

Coconut Kisses

Coffee Kisses

INGREDIENTS
Biscuits:
100g (4 oz) plain flour
50g (2 oz) margarine
50g (2 oz) caster sugar
1 egg yolk
a little milk
½ tsp baking powder
pinch of salt

Topping:
125g (4 oz) desiccated coconut
50g (2 oz) caster sugar
1 egg white
glacé cherries

METHOD
For the biscuits, sieve the flour, salt and baking powder together. Mix in the sugar. Rub in the fat and mix with the beaten egg yolk. Add a little milk if required. Roll out the dough and cut out shapes with a 3cm (1½ in) cutter. Place on greased baking trays.

For the topping, whisk the egg white until it is stiff. Add the sugar and whisk again. Fold in the coconut. Spread the mixture onto each biscuit and top it with a quarter of a cherry if desired. Bake them for 25 to 30 minutes until the biscuits are nicely browned. This recipe makes 24 biscuits. Oven 180°C/350°F. Gas 4.

INGREDIENTS
Biscuits
225g (8 oz) self-raising flour
75g (3 oz) caster sugar
75g (3 oz) margarine
1 egg
½ tsp coffee essence or
about 2 tsp instant coffee

Filling:
100g (4 oz) icing sugar
50g (2 oz) butter
1 tsp coffee essence or 1 tsp instant coffee dissolved in 1 tsp hot water

METHOD
For the biscuits, rub the margarine into the flour and sugar. Mix in the beaten egg and coffee flavouring. Roll the dough into small balls and place on greased baking sheets. Bake them in a moderate oven for 15 to 20 minutes.

To make the filling, cream the butter until it is soft. Gradually add the sieved icing sugar and cream them together. Add the coffee flavouring and beat well.

When the biscuits are cool, sandwich them together with the filling.
Oven 180°C/350°F. Gas 4.

Coffee Walnut Biscuits

INGREDIENTS
100g (4 oz) plain flour
100g (4 oz) butter
50g (2 oz) caster sugar
50g (2 oz) chopped walnuts
2 tsp instant coffee

METHOD
Beat the butter and sugar together, then add the rest of the ingredients. Place small teaspoonfuls of the mixture on greased baking sheets leaving plenty of room for the biscuits to spread. Bake for 15 to 20 minutes. If they are evenly spooned, this recipe should make 18 to 20 biscuits.
Oven 190°C/375°F. Gas 5.

Cornish Ginger Fairings

INGREDIENTS
175g (6 oz) self-raising flour
125g (4 oz) butter
125g (4 oz) caster sugar
1 tsp ground ginger
1 tbsp golden syrup
pinch of bicarbonate of soda

METHOD
Melt the butter, sugar and syrup in a pan. Then mix in the dry ingredients. Roll the dough into small balls and place them on greased baking trays. Bake them in a hot oven for 10 to 15 minutes or until they are golden brown.
Oven 200°C/400°F. Gas 6.

Coupland Biscuits

Crescent Biscuits

INGREDIENTS
100g (4 oz) plain flour
100g (4 oz) butter or margarine
50g (2 oz) rolled oats
50g (2 oz) desiccated coconut
50g (2 oz) caster sugar
1 tbsp golden syrup
1 tsp bicarbonate of soda
2 tsp hot water

METHOD
Mix the butter, sugar and syrup together until they are soft and creamy. Add the dry ingredients and mix them all together with the bicarbonate of soda and water.

Roll the dough into small balls, place them on greased baking sheets and flatten them. Bake them in a moderate oven for about 20 minutes or until they are golden brown.
Oven 180°C/350°F. Gas 4.

INGREDIENTS
200g (7 oz) plain flour
175g (6 oz) fat (half butter, half margarine)
75g (3 oz) ground almonds
50g (2 oz) caster sugar
few drops of vanilla essence
caster sugar for sprinkling

METHOD
Rub the flour and fat together. Add the sugar, almonds and essence. Knead the mixture to a stiff paste.

Roll it out to a thickness of 1cm (½ in). Cut it into crescent shapes. Bake them in a slow oven for 30 minutes. Sprinkle them with caster sugar.
Oven 150°C/300°F. Gas 2.

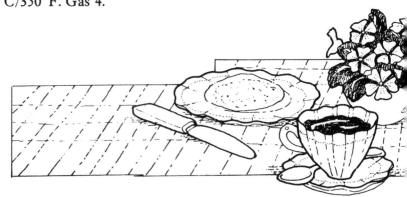

Crisps

INGREDIENTS
175g (6 oz) margarine
125g (4 oz) self-raising flour
125g (4 oz) soft brown sugar
125g (4 oz) bran buds
1 tsp baking powder

METHOD
Cream the margarine and sugar together. Add the sieved flour and baking powder and then the bran buds. Knead them together.

Roll the dough into small balls and bake them on greased baking sheets for about 15 minutes or until they are golden brown. This recipe makes 36 biscuits.
Oven 180°C/350°F. Gas 4.

Creston Drops

INGREDIENTS
225g (8 oz) plain flour
125g (4 oz) butter
125g (4 oz) raisins
125g (4 oz) chopped walnuts
50g (2 oz) caster sugar
6 tbsp milk
3 squares chocolate
2 eggs
1 tsp salt
½ tsp bicarbonate of soda

METHOD
Cream the butter and sugar. Add the eggs, then the melted chocolate, nuts and raisins. Sieve the flour with the salt and bicarbonate of soda and add them to the mixture alternately with the milk.

Drop spoonfuls onto a greased baking sheet and flatten them with a spoon. Bake for 10 to 15 minutes.
Oven 200°C/400°F. Gas 6.

Crunchies

INGREDIENTS
100g (4 oz) self-raising flour
100g (4 oz) rolled oats
100g (4 oz) granulated sugar
100g (4 oz) desiccated coconut
100g (4 oz) margarine
1 tbsp golden syrup
1 tsp bicarbonate of soda
1 tbsp tepid water

METHOD
Dissolve the bicarbonate of soda in the water. Melt the fat and syrup in a pan and mix all the ingredients together.
Roll the dough into small balls. Bake them on a greased baking tray for about 20 minutes.
Oven 150°C/300°F. Gas 2.

Crunchy Biscuits

INGREDIENTS
Biscuits:
100g (4 oz) self-raising flour
100g (4 oz) rolled oats
100g (4 oz) butter or margarine
75g (3 oz) caster sugar
1 tbsp golden syrup
pinch of salt
pinch of bicarbonate of soda

Topping:
175g (6 oz) cooking chocolate

METHOD
Cream the butter, sugar and syrup, then mix in the dry ingredients. Roll the dough into small balls. Place them on a baking tray and press them flat with a fork. Bake them for 15 to 20 minutes. When the biscuits are cool, cover them with melted chocolate.
Oven 180°C/350°F. Gas 4.

Cumberland Snaps

INGREDIENTS
225g (8 oz) plain flour
225g (8 oz) margarine
125g (4 oz) caster sugar
50g (2 oz) rolled oats
2 tbsp golden syrup
1 tsp ground ginger
1 tsp bicarbonate of soda
1 tbsp hot water

METHOD
Melt the sugar, margarine and syrup over a low heat. Dissolve the bicarbonate of soda in the hot water, then mix it in together with all the other ingredients.

Roll the dough into small balls of about the size of a walnut. Place them on a greased tin and bake them for 20 to 25 minutes until they are golden brown.
Oven 160°C/325°F. Gas 3.

Curly Peters

INGREDIENTS
Plain mixture:
225g (8 oz) plain flour
125g (4 oz) margarine
125g (4 oz) caster sugar
1 egg
1 tsp baking powder

Chocolate mixture:
175g (6 oz) plain flour sieved with
   50g (2 oz) cocoa powder
125g (4 oz) caster sugar
125g (4 oz) margarine
1 egg
1 tsp baking powder

METHOD
For both mixtures rub the margarine into the flour, then add the sugar and baking powder. Bind them together with the egg to make a stiff paste.

Roll out each mixture separately, then lay the chocolate mixture on top of the plain one. Roll them up like a Swiss roll. Cut the roll into 0.5cm (¼ in) slices and lay them on a greased tray. Bake them for 20 to 25 minutes or until they are pale brown.
Oven 150-160°/300-325°F. Gas 2- 3.

D

Danish Specier Biscuits

INGREDIENTS
225g (8 oz) plain flour
175g (6 oz) butter or margarine
75g (3 oz) icing sugar
25g (1 oz) blanched chopped
   almonds
granulated sugar

METHOD
Measure the butter, flour, sifted icing sugar and almonds into a bowl and mix them together. Shape the dough into two sausages about 5cm (2 in) thick and roll them in granulated sugar until they are completely covered. Place in a fridge until they are firm.

Cut the dough into 0.5cm (¼ in) thick slices and arrange them on an ungreased baking tray.

Bake them in a hot oven for about 8 to 10 minutes until they are light brown around the edges. This recipe makes 40 biscuits.
Oven 200°C/400°F. Gas 6.

Date Slices

INGREDIENTS
100g (4 oz) self-raising flour
100g (4 oz) rolled oats
100g (4 oz) caster sugar
100g (4 oz) butter or margarine
100g (4 oz) dates

METHOD
Boil the dates with sufficient water to barely cover them. Cook them until the mixture resembles thick jam. More water may be added or boiled off if necessary.

Mix the rest of the ingredients well together. Press half of this mixture into a greased Swiss roll tin, spread the dates on top, and cover them with the remainder of the mixture.

Bake in a moderate oven for approximately 20 minutes or until the surface is nicely browned. Cut it into fingers while it is still hot, but leave it in the tin until it has cooled.
Oven 180°C/350°F. Gas 4.

Date Sticks

INGREDIENTS
450g (1 lb) chopped stoned dates
175g (6 oz) self-raising flour
50g (2 oz) caster sugar
50g (2 oz) chopped walnuts
25g (1 oz) butter
2 eggs
1 tbsp hot water
pinch of salt
caster sugar for sprinkling

METHOD
Beat together the eggs, sugar, salt and melted butter. Mix in the dates and walnuts, then add the flour and hot water.

Spread the mixture into two well greased and floured Swiss roll tins. Bake for 20 to 25 minutes. Cut them into fingers and sprinkle them with caster sugar.
Oven 190°C/375°F. Gas 5.

Dream Cookies

INGREDIENTS
150g (5 oz) plain flour
125g (4 oz) soft margarine
75g (3 oz) caster sugar
½ tsp baking powder
1-2 drops of vanilla essence
pinch of salt
blanched almonds

METHOD
Cream margarine and sugar. Sieve the flour together with the salt and baking powder and blend them with the creamed mixture. Add the vanilla essence.

Roll the dough into small balls. Top each one with an almond and place them on a greased tray. Bake them in a moderate oven for 15 to 20 minutes or until they are pale gold.
Oven 180°C/350°F. Gas 4.

Drop Cookies

INGREDIENTS
175g (6 oz) plain flour
100g (4 oz) butter or margarine
100g (4 oz) chocolate chips
75g (3 oz) caster sugar
25g (1 oz) brown sugar
1 egg
1 tsp bicarbonate of soda
few drops of vanilla essence
pinch of salt

METHOD
Sift together the flour, bicarbonate
of soda and salt onto a plate.
Cream the butter and both sugars
in a basin until they are soft and
light. Gradually beat in the lightly
beaten egg and vanilla essence. Stir
in half of the sifted flour mixture.
Beat well to get a smooth dough.
Then add the remaining flour and
the chocolate chips. Stir to blend
the ingredients thoroughly.
   Take rounded teaspoonfuls of
the mixture and place them on
greased baking trays — about 12 to
a tray. Bake in a moderate oven for
12 to 15 minutes. Lift them
carefully onto a cooling tray so that
they lie flat.
Oven 160°C/325°F. Gas 3.

E

Easter Biscuits

caster sugar, then return them to the oven.
Oven 180°C/350°F. Gas 4.

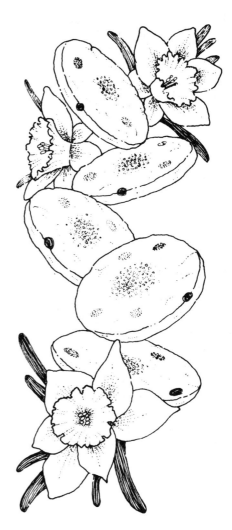

INGREDIENTS
Biscuits:
175g (6 oz) plain flour
75g (3 oz) butter
75g (3 oz) caster sugar
50g (2 oz) currants
15g (½ oz) candied peel
pinch of mixed spice
1 egg yolk
a little milk

Glazing:
1 egg white
caster sugar

METHOD
Cream the butter, add the sugar and beat the mixture until it is fluffy. Add the egg yolk, spice, fruit and flour. Then mix to a stiff dough with the milk. Roll the dough out thinly. Cut into rounds and place them on a greased baking sheet.
    Bake them in a moderate oven for 15 to 20 minutes. After 10 minutes, brush them with the egg white and sprinkle them with

Easter Bunny Biscuits

Bake the biscuits near the top of the oven for 15 to 18 minutes. Leave them to cool on a cake rack. Oven 190°C/375°F. Gas 5.

INGREDIENTS
Biscuits:
225g (8 oz) plain flour
100g (4 oz) caster sugar
75g (3 oz) soft margarine
25g (1 oz) currants
1 egg
2 tsp mixed spice
pinch of salt

Coating:
egg white
desiccated coconut

METHOD
Cream the fat and sugar until they are light and fluffy. Beat in the egg thoroughly, then fold in the sieved flour, salt, and spice. Add the currants and mix them well to form a dough.

Roll it out on a floured board to a thickness of 0.5cm (¼ in). Cut out the biscuits with a rabbit-shaped cutter. Brush them with egg white and dip them in the coconut. Add a currant on each one to represent an eye.

Place the biscuits on a baking sheet which has been brushed with melted cooking fat and lightly floured.

F

Finnish Shortbread

Firelighter Biscuits

INGREDIENTS
Biscuits:
350g (12 oz) plain flour
225g (8 oz) butter
125g (4 oz) caster sugar
1 egg yolk

Coating:
2-3 egg yolks
chopped almonds
coarse granulated sugar

METHOD
Rub the butter into the flour and add the sugar. Make them into a dough with the egg yolk and knead it lightly. Roll the dough into lengths the thickness of your little finger and cut it into 1cm (½ in) long pieces.

Dip the pieces into the beaten egg yolk, then roll them in a mixture of chopped almonds and sugar. Bake them in a moderate oven for 20 minutes until they are golden brown.
Oven 180°C/350°F. Gas 4.

INGREDIENTS
225g (8 oz) rolled oats
125g (4 oz) brown sugar
125g (4 oz) margarine
25g (1 oz) desiccated coconut
1 tbsp golden syrup
pinch of baking powder

METHOD
Melt the fat and syrup together, add the dry ingredients and mix them together thoroughly. Press the dough into a Swiss roll tin so that it is 1cm (½ in) thick. Bake it for 20 to 30 minutes. Cut it into fingers when it is cold.
Oven 180°C./350°F. Gas 4.

Flaked Almond Biscuits

INGREDIENTS
100g (4 oz) self-raising flour
100g (4 oz) caster sugar
100g (4 oz) margarine or butter
100g (4 oz) rolled oats
25g (1 oz) almonds
2 tsp dark treacle
1 tsp bicarbonate of soda
4 tbsp boiling water

METHOD
Cream the butter and sugar. Add the treacle, then mix in the flour, oats and nuts. Dissolve the bicarbonate of soda in the water and stir this well into the mixture.

Roll teaspoonfuls of the mixture into balls. Put them on greased sheets, allowing room for the biscuits to spread. Bake them for 15 minutes. This recipe makes 48 biscuits.
Oven 180°C/350°F. Gas 4.

Florentines

INGREDIENTS
Biscuits:
100g (4 oz) flaked almonds
75g (3 oz) caster sugar
75g (3 oz) mixed glacé cherries, raisins and candied peel
1 (scant) tbsp self-raising flour
2 tsp butter
150 ml (¼ pt) cream

Topping:
175g (6 oz) plain block chocolate

METHOD
Heat the cream and sugar slowly in a thick saucepan until the sugar has dissolved. Bring to the boil, then tip in the chopped fruit, nuts, butter and flour. Remove from the heat and mix thoroughly with a wooden spoon.

Line a baking sheet with baking parchment. Place small tea-spoonfuls of the mixture 15cm (6 in) apart on the baking sheet. Bake them for about 10 minutes, or until they are nicely brown. Remove the biscuits at once from the sheet and cool them on a rack.

For the topping, melt the chocolate in a basin over hot water. When the biscuits are cold, spread their undersides with melted chocolate and mark the chocolate with a fork. Leave them upside down on a flat surface to dry.
Oven 190°C/375°F. Gas 5.

Freezer Biscuits

INGREDIENTS

200g (7 oz) plain flour
200g (7 oz) caster sugar
100g (4 oz) butter or soft
  margarine
1 egg
1 tsp baking powder
½ tsp salt

METHOD

Mix together the egg and sugar.
Sift the flour into a bowl with the
baking powder and salt and add
any flavouring (see variations).
Melt the butter or use soft
margarine and add this to the
mixture to make a soft dough.

Knead it lightly then form it into
a sausage shape 2.5cm (1 in) in
diameter. Wrap it in grease-proof
paper and foil and keep it in the
freezer or fridge until it is needed.
Cut off slices about 0.5cm (¼ in)
thick and bake them in a moderate
oven for 15 to 20 minutes.
Oven 180°C/350°F. Gas 4.

VARIATIONS

(1) 1 tsp vanilla essence and 50g
    (2 oz) chopped walnuts
(2) 1 tsp almond essence and 50g
    (2 oz) chopped almonds
(3) 1 tsp ground ginger and 50g
    (2 oz) crystallized ginger
(4) 50g (2 oz) grated chocolate and
    1 tsp vanilla essence
(5) 1 tbsp instant coffee and 50g
    (2 oz) chopped walnuts
(6) Grated rind of lemon and 50g
    (2 oz) currants
(7) 1 tsp vanilla essence and 1 tbsp
    instant coffee
(8) Use soft brown sugar instead of
    caster sugar and add 1 tsp
    vanilla and 50g (2 oz) chopped
    raisins

Fruity Brittles

INGREDIENTS
150g (5 oz) butter or magarine
125g (4 oz) self-raising flour
125g (4 oz) caster sugar
125g (4 oz) crushed cornflakes
125g (4 oz) chopped mixed fruit
50g (2 oz) chopped walnuts
1 egg
pinch of salt

METHOD
Rub the butter into the flour, then mix in the sugar, salt, fruit and nuts. Beat the egg and stir it into the mixture.

Roll small pieces (ping-pong ball size) of the mixture in the crushed cornflakes. Place them on greased baking trays leaving room for them to spread. Bake them for 10 to 15 minutes.
Oven 200°C/400°F. Gas 6.

Fruity Snaps

INGREDIENTS
150g (5 oz) self-raising flour
50g (2 oz) sultanas
50g (2 oz) margarine
25g (1 oz) caster sugar
4 tbsp golden syrup

METHOD
Place the sultanas, sugar, margarine and syrup in a pan and warm them over a low heat. Take care that the mixture does not overheat. Remove it from the heat, add the flour and beat well.

Place small tablespoonfuls of the mixture well apart on greased baking sheets. Bake them in a moderate oven for about 12 to 15 minutes until they are golden brown. Allow them to set before removing them from the trays, but do not leave them for too long or they will stick.
Oven 180°C/350°F. Gas 4.

G

Garibaldi Biscuits

greased baking trays for 15 minutes or until they are golden brown. Sprinkle them with caster sugar. Oven 200°C/400°F. Gas 6.

INGREDIENTS
200g (7 oz) self-raising flour
75g-100g (3-4 oz) currants
50g (2 oz) caster sugar
50g (2 oz) butter or margarine
25g (1 oz) cornflour
1 egg yolk
pinch of salt
a little milk
caster sugar for sprinkling

METHOD
Sieve the flour, cornflour, sugar and salt into a basin. Rub in the butter until the mixture is the consistency of bread crumbs. Mix it to a stiffish dough with the egg yolk and milk.

Turn it onto a floured board and roll it out to a thin oblong. Trim the edges then sprinkle one half of the dough with the currants. Fold over the other half of the dough and press the edges well together. Roll the dough lightly with a floured rolling pin until it is about 0.25cm (⅛ in) thick. Cut it into 0.5cm (2 in) squares. Bake them on

German Almond Biscuits

INGREDIENTS
225g (8 oz) butter
175g (6 oz) caster sugar
125g (4 oz) plain flour
125g (4 oz) self-raising flour
1 egg
raspberry jam
flaked almonds
1 tsp sugar for glazing

METHOD
Cream the butter and sugar and add the beaten egg (keeping back a small quantity for glazing). Stir in the flour and mix well.

Divide the mixture into two and cover the bottom of a well greased round 18cm (7 in) tin, with one half. Spread this with raspberry jam. Then cover the jam with the remaining mixture.

Add a teaspoonful of sugar to the remainder of the egg. Brush this over the top then sprinkle it with flaked almonds. Bake it in a slow oven for 45 minutes. Cut it into slices when it is almost cold.

This is equally good if the jam is omitted, but the mixture should then be spread over a larger tin. Oven 150°C/300°F. Gas 2.

German Biscuits

INGREDIENTS
Biscuits:
200g (7 oz) plain flour
125g (4 oz) caster sugar
125g (4 oz) butter or margarine
½ tsp baking powder
½ tsp ground cinnamon
1 egg

Filling:
raspberry jam

Icing:
150g (6 oz) icing sugar
1½ tbsp water

Decoration:
glacé cherries

METHOD
For the biscuits, sieve the flour, baking powder and cinnamon, then rub the butter into the flour. Mix in all the dry ingredients. Mix them to a stiff paste with the egg.

Roll the dough out to a thickness of 0.25cm (⅛ in) and cut it into rounds. Bake in a moderate oven for 10 to 15 minutes.

When the biscuits are cold, sandwich them together with the raspberry jam.

To make the icing, mix the sieved icing sugar with the water and beat them until they are smooth.

Ice the tops of the biscuits, then decorate them with glacé cherries.

These biscuits taste even better if they are made the day before they are eaten.

Oven 180°C/350°F. Gas 4.

Ginger Biscuits

INGREDIENTS

225g (8 oz) self-raising flour
125g (4 oz) caster sugar
125g (4 oz) margarine
1 tbsp treacle
1 tbsp golden syrup
1 tsp ground ginger
1 tsp bicarbonate of soda
a little hot water

METHOD

Cream the margarine and sugar in a bowl. Warm the treacle and syrup and add them to the creamed mixture with the sieved flour and ginger. Dissolve the bicarbonate of soda in a little hot water and stir it into the mixture. Mix them well.

Roll the dough into balls and place them on greased baking trays. Bake them in a moderate oven for 15 minutes.

Oven 180°C/350°F. Gas 4.

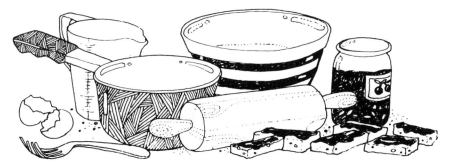

Ginger Ruffles

INGREDIENTS
100g (4 oz) self-raising flour
50g (2 oz) caster sugar
50g (2 oz) margarine
2 tbsp golden syrup
1 tsp ground ginger
½ tsp bicarbonate of soda

METHOD
Sieve the flour, bicarbonate of soda and ginger, rub in the margarine and add the sugar. Warm the syrup and mix them well together.

Divide the dough into two pieces and form each one into a long sausage. Place each one in the middle of a baking tray. Bake them at the top of a moderate oven for about 20 minutes. Remove them from the oven and cut them into strips while they are still warm.
Oven 180°C/350°F. Gas 4.

Ginger Snaps

INGREDIENTS
225g (8 oz) plain flour
125g (4 oz) margarine
4 tbsp golden syrup
125g (4 oz) caster sugar
1 tsp ground ginger
½ tsp bicarbonate of soda
1 egg yolk
pinch of salt
a little milk

METHOD
Melt the margarine and syrup together. Sieve the flour, salt and ginger into a basin and stir in the sugar. Blend them with the melted margarine and syrup and the beaten egg yolk. Dissolve the bicarbonate of soda in a little warm milk and add it to the mixture.

Turn the dough onto a floured board and knead it until it is smooth. Roll it out thinly on a sugared board and cut it into rounds. Place them on a greased and floured baking sheet and bake them for 15 to 20 minutes. Allow them to set on the baking tray then leave them to cool on a wire tray.
Oven 190°C/375°F. Gas 5.

Gipsy Creams

When the biscuits are cool, sandwich them together in pairs with the filling.
Oven 180°C/350°F. Gas 4.

INGREDIENTS
Biscuits:
125g (4 oz) self-raising flour
50g (2 oz) rolled oats
50g (2 oz) lard
50g (2 oz) margarine
50g (2 oz) caster sugar
1 tbsp chocolate or cocoa powder
2 tsp golden syrup dissolved in 1
   tbsp hot water

Filling:
50g (2 oz) icing sugar
25g (1 oz) butter
1 tbsp chocolate powder
few drops of vanilla essence

METHOD
For the biscuits, cream together the lard, margarine and sugar, then mix in all the other ingredients. Roll the dough into balls about the size of a large cherry.

Place them on greased baking trays and flatten them with a fork which has been dipped in water. Bake them for about 20 minutes and leave them on trays to cool.

To make the filling, cream the butter until it is soft. Gradually add the sieved icing sugar and cream them to a smooth consistency. Add the chocolate powder and vanilla essence and beat well.

Gipsy Crisps

INGREDIENTS
225g (8 oz) self-raising flour
150g (5 oz) margarine
125g (4 oz) sugar
75g (3 oz) cornflakes
2 tbsp golden syrup
1 tsp bicarbonate of soda
2 tsp boiling water

METHOD
Crush the cornflakes and mix them with the dry ingredients. Melt the margarine and syrup and add them to the dry mixture. Finally, dissolve the bicarbonate of soda in the boiling water and add them to the mixture. Roll the dough into small round balls, place them on greased baking sheets and bake them in a slow oven for 20 to 25 minutes.
Oven 150°C/300°F. Gas 2.

Grantham Ginger Drops

INGREDIENTS
100g (4 oz) self-raising flour
100g (4 oz) butter or margarine
100g (4 oz) caster sugar
2 tsp ground ginger

METHOD
Lightly cream the fat and sugar together until they are soft, but do not cream them too much. Add the ginger, then the flour, and work the mixture to a stiff dough.
Roll the dough into small balls and place them, spaced well apart, on ungreased baking trays. Bake them for 30 to 40 minutes. This recipe makes 24 biscuits.
Oven 125°C/250°F. Gas ½.

VARIATIONS
(1) Plain: omit the ginger
(2) Chocolate: substitute 2 rounded tsp cocoa powder for the ginger

Grasmere Gingerbread

INGREDIENTS
450g (1 lb) plain flour
225g (8 oz) soft brown sugar
225g (8 oz) margarine or butter
2 tsp ground ginger
1 tsp bicarbonate of soda
1 tsp cream of tartar

METHOD
Mix together the dry ingredients, then rub in the fat. Press the mixture into a 25 x 30cm (10 x 12 in) flat tin. Bake for about 45 minutes. Allow the gingerbread to cool slightly before cutting it into pieces.
Oven 150°C/300°F. Gas 2.

Ground Rice Cookies

INGREDIENTS
100g (4 oz) self-raising flour
100g (4 oz) ground rice
100g (4 oz) caster sugar
100g (4 oz) margarine
1 egg
sugar for coating

METHOD
Rub the margarine into the mixed dry ingredients and blend them into a dough with the beaten egg. Roll the dough into small balls and dip them in sugar.

Place them on greased baking sheets and flatten them slightly with a fork. Bake them in a moderate oven for 15 to 20 minutes.
Oven 180°C/350°F. Gas 4.

H

Highlanders

INGREDIENTS
100g (4 oz) butter
75g (3 oz) self-raising flour
75g (3 oz) plain flour
50g (2 oz) icing sugar
25g (1 oz) demerara sugar

METHOD
Cream the icing sugar and butter until they are very light. Work in the flours and knead thoroughly. Form the mixture into a sausage. Roll it in the demerara sugar. Place it on something flat and put it in the fridge for at least one hour.

Cut into 0.5cm (¼ in) slices, and place the biscuits on an ungreased tray. Bake them for about 10 minutes. Be careful that the edges do not burn. Cool them on a tray. This recipe makes about 20 biscuits.
Oven 180°C/350°F. Gas 4.

Honey Biscuits

INGREDIENTS
100g (4 oz) unsalted butter
100g (4 oz) plain flour
100g (4 oz) sugar lumps
50g (2 oz) caster sugar
6 tbsp clear honey
1 tsp bicarbonate of soda
1 egg yolk

METHOD
Melt the butter and pour it into a large bowl. As it begins to cool, stir in the honey, caster sugar, bicarbonate of soda and egg yolk. Add the flour gradually and mix to make a firm dough.

Roll rounded teaspoonfuls of the mixture into balls on a floured surface. Coarsely crush the sugar lumps and dip the top of each ball into it. Place the balls on a baking tray lined with baking parchment and bake for 12 minutes.
Oven 200°C/400°F. Gas 6.

I

Iced Ginger Shortcake

heating the mixed ingredients over a low heat. Pour it over the shortcake while it is still hot. Cut it into fingers before it cools.
Oven 160°C/325°F. Gas 3.

INGREDIENTS
Base:
150g (5 oz) plain flour
125g (4 oz) butter or margarine
50g (2 oz) caster sugar
1 tsp ground ginger
1 tsp baking powder

Icing:
100g (4 oz) caster sugar
50g (2 oz) butter or margarine
1 tbsp golden syrup
1 tsp ground ginger

METHOD
Sieve together the flour, baking powder and ginger. Cream the butter and sugar until they are light and fluffy. Mix the dry ingredients into the creamed mixture.

Spread the mixture into the tin and cook it for 45 minutes until it is golden brown.

Meanwhile, prepare the icing by

Iced Peppermint Biscuits

should be quite thick. Spread the biscuits with the icing and leave it to set.

Coat the biscuits with the melted chocolate and decorate them with the vermicelli.

Oven 160°C/325°. Gas 3.

INGREDIENTS

Biscuits:
75g (3 oz) plain flour
50g (2 oz) butter
25g (1 oz) sugar

Icing:
100g (4 oz) icing sugar
approx 1 tbsp water
few drops of peppermint essence
few drops of green food colouring

Topping:
225g (8 oz) cooking chocolate
chocolate vermicelli

METHOD

Sieve the flour, rub in the butter, and add the sugar. Knead them until the mixture is smooth. Roll it out thinly and cut it into shapes. Place the biscuits on a greased baking sheet. Bake them for 10 to 15 minutes. Allow them to cool before removing them from the baking sheet.

Prepare the icing by adding the peppermint essence and food colouring to the water. Mix in the sieved icing sugar and beat them to a smooth consistency. Not all the water may be required as the icing

Iced Raspberry Biscuits

INGREDIENTS
Biscuits:
200g (7 oz) plain flour
75g (3 oz) margarine
75g (3 oz) caster sugar
1 egg
pinch of salt

Filling:
raspberry jam

Icing:
100g (4 oz) icing sugar
1 tbsp water

METHOD
Cream the margarine and sugar,
add the egg, then stir in the flour
and salt. Knead them together. Roll
out the dough and cut it into
rounds with a medium-size cutter.
Bake them for 8 to 10 minutes.
   When they are cool, sandwich
them together with the raspberry
jam.
   To make the icing, mix the
sieved icing sugar with the water
and beat them to a smooth
consistency. Spread the icing over
the tops of the biscuits and leave it
to set.
Oven 200°C/400°F. Gas 6.

J

Joyce's Biscuits

Jumbles

Joyce's Biscuits

INGREDIENTS
125g (4 oz) self-raising flour
125g (4 oz) margarine
75g (3 oz) caster sugar
50g (2 oz) rolled oats
1 tbsp golden syrup
1 tsp bicarbonate of soda
2 tsp water
few drops of vanilla essence

METHOD
Melt the margarine and syrup in a pan with the water. Add them to the dry ingredients. Roll the mixture into small balls and place them on greased trays. Bake them for 10 to 15 minutes or until they are golden brown.
Oven 190°C/375°F. Gas 5.

Jumbles

INGREDIENTS
225g (8 oz) plain flour
225g (8 oz) caster sugar
175g (6 oz) butter
1 large egg
lemon rind
caster sugar for dusting

METHOD
Rub the butter into the flour, add the sugar and the finely grated lemon rind and stir in the beaten egg.
Roll the dough into long rolls. Cut them into 10cm (4 in) lengths and make them into wheel or 'S' shapes. Bake them in a moderate oven for 15 to 20 minutes or until evenly browned. Dust them with caster sugar immediately.
Oven 180°C/350°F. Gas 4.

K

Kelvin Crisps

(2) Topped with a dab of melted chocolate and half a glacé cherry.

(3) Sandwiched together with apricot jam.

INGREDIENTS

100g (4 oz) plain flour
100g (4 oz) butter or margarine
75g (3 oz) caster sugar
75g (3 oz) desiccated coconut
1 egg
½ tsp ground cinnamon
½ tsp baking powder

METHOD

Sieve the flour, cinnamon and baking powder into a bowl, then rub in the butter. Add the remainder of the dry ingredients and mix them together with the well beaten egg to make a fairly stiff dough.

Roll the dough out to a thickness of 0.5cm (¼ in). Stamp it out into small rounds and place them on a greased baking sheet. Bake them for 15 minutes in a moderate oven. Oven 180°C/350°F. Gas 4.

VARIATIONS

When they are cold, Serve them:
(1) Plain

King Haakon Biscuits

INGREDIENTS
225g (8 oz) plain flour
225g (8 oz) butter
125g (4 oz) icing sugar
50g (2 oz) chopped walnuts
50g (2 oz) glacé cherries
pinch of salt

METHOD
Sieve the icing sugar into the flour
and rub the butter into the flour
and icing sugar. Add the other
ingredients. Form the dough into a
good shaped roll. Wrap it in foil
and put it in the fridge to harden.
   When the dough is very firm,
slice it into rounds. Place them on
a greased baking tray, and bake
them in a slow oven for 20 to 25
minutes.
Oven 150°C/300°F. Gas 2.

Kourabiédes (Greek Butter Cookies)

INGREDIENTS
275g (10 oz) plain flour
225g (8 oz) butter
75g (3 oz) caster sugar
2 tbsp ouzo
½ tsp baking powder
¼ tsp vanilla essence
1 egg yolk
40 whole cloves
icing sugar
rosewater

METHOD
Cream the butter and sugar. Beat
in the ouzo, vanilla essence and egg
yolk. Sift the flour and baking
powder and add them to the
mixture. Mix well to make a firm
dough.
   Form rounded teaspoonfuls of
the dough into balls and place
them on a baking tray lined with
baking parchment. Flatten them
slightly and spike each cookie with
a clove. Bake for 20 minutes.
   Transfer the biscuits immediately
to a cooling rack and, while they
are still hot, sprinkle them with
icing sugar and rosewater. This

recipe makes approximately 40 biscuits.

Kourabiédes are usually served at Christmas.

Oven 190°C/375°F. Gas 5.

Kringles

INGREDIENTS
225g (8 oz) plain flour
225g (8 oz) caster sugar
125g (4 oz) butter
2 tsp baking powder
2 tsp caraway seeds
3 tbsp brandy
1 egg
caster sugar for sprinkling

METHOD
Sieve 175g (6 oz) of the flour with the baking powder. Cream the butter and sugar and beat in the egg, brandy and caraway seeds. Stir in the sieved flour, then add enough of the spare 50g (2 oz) of flour to make a stiff dough that you can handle. Chill it thoroughly.

Roll it out to a thickness of 0.25cm (⅛ in). Cut it into shapes and put them on ungreased trays. Sprinkle them with the caster sugar and bake them for 15 minutes. This recipe makes 48 biscuits. Oven 190°C/375°F. Gas 5.

L

Lace Biscuits

Lancashire Nuts

INGREDIENTS
100g (4 oz) margarine
100g (4 oz) caster sugar
100g (4 oz) chopped almonds
50g (2 oz) plain flour
juice of 1 lemon
pinch of salt

METHOD
Cream the margarine, sugar and
lemon juice. Add the almonds then
stir in the flour and salt. Mix the
dough well.

Break off pieces the size of a
walnut and put them on greased
trays. Space them well apart as
they will spread. Press them with a
fork and bake them for 15 to 20
minutes. Do not remove them from
the trays until they are cold.
Oven 180°C/350°F. Gas 4.

INGREDIENTS
Biscuits:
100g (4 oz) plain flour
100g (4 oz) cornflour
100g (4 oz) caster sugar
100g (4 oz) butter
1 egg
1 tbsp baking powder

Filling:
100g (4 oz) icing sugar
50g (2 oz) butter
few drops vanilla essence

METHOD
For the biscuits, cream the butter
and sugar. Add the egg and beat
them together. Then add all the
dry ingredients. Mix them to a
paste. Place teaspoonfuls of the
dough on a greased tin and bake
them for 8 to 10 minutes until they
are golden.

To make the filling, cream the
butter until it is soft. Gradually
add the sieved icing sugar and
cream them together. Add the

vanilla essence and beat the mixture well. When they are cold, sandwich the biscuits together in pairs with the filling.
Oven 180°C/350°F. Gas 4.

Lemon Crescents

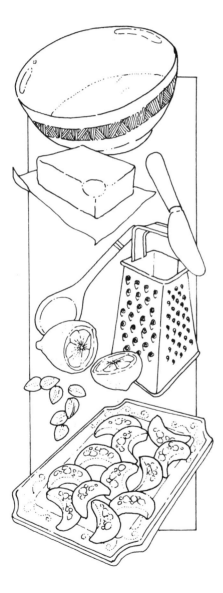

INGREDIENTS
100g (4 oz) plain flour
50g (2 oz) butter
50g (2 oz) caster sugar
rind and juice of ½ lemon
1 egg
chopped almonds

METHOD
Rub the grated lemon rind and the sugar in a basin until the sugar is yellow. Rub the butter into the flour until it is free from lumps. Add the lemon juice and sugar and sufficient egg to blend them together.

Roll the dough out thinly and cut it into crescent shapes. Place them on a greased tray. Brush them over with beaten egg and sprinkle them with chopped almonds. Bake them in a moderate oven for 20 minutes.
Oven 180°C/350°F. Gas 4.

Lemon Fudge Biscuits

INGREDIENTS
Base:
225g (8 oz) plain "tea" biscuits
125g (4 oz) margarine or butter
50g (2 oz) desiccated coconut
200g (7 oz) condensed milk
grated rind of ½ lemon

Icing:
150g (6 oz) icing sugar
1½ tbsp lemon juice
few drops yellow food colouring

METHOD
For the base, crush the biscuits
then add the coconut and lemon
rind. Melt the butter and add the
milk. Mix together all the
ingredients. Press the mixture into
a Swiss roll tin.

To prepare the icing, add the
yellow food colouring to the lemon
juice and mix in the sieved icing
sugar.

Spread the icing over the base
and leave it to set. Cut the biscuits
into shapes.

M

Macaroons

INGREDIENTS
225g (8 oz) caster sugar
100g (4 oz) ground almonds
25g (1 oz) ground rice
2 egg whites
a few split almonds
rice paper
egg white for glazing

METHOD
Whisk the egg whites until they are stiff, then fold in the ground almonds, ground rice and sugar.
  Line baking trays with rice paper. Place small heaps of the mixture on the baking trays. Space them out so that there is room for them to spread. Top each one with a split almond and glaze them with egg white. Bake them in a moderate oven for 25 to 30 minutes.
Oven 180°C/350°F. Gas 4.

Ma' Moule

INGREDIENTS
75g (3 oz) butter
75g (3 oz) semolina
35g (1½ oz) chopped walnuts
35g (1½ oz) caster sugar
25g (1 oz) plain flour
2 tsp boiling water
½ tsp rose flower water
½ tsp orange flower water
fine sugar for sprinkling

METHOD
Make a dough from the semolina, flour, butter and boiling water. Knead it lightly, cover it, and leave it overnight.
  The next day, roll the dough into small balls. Make a small dent in the centre of each one with your finger tip. Fill this with a mixture of the pounded chopped walnuts, sugar, rose and orange flower water. Pinch the edges together to cover the filling and then flatten them with the palm of your hand. Bake them for 10 to 15 minutes until they are golden. While they are still hot, sprinkle them with fine sugar.
Oven 190°C/375°F. Gas 5.

Marzipan Biscuits

oven for 8 to 10 minutes or until they are golden. Cool them on a wire rack.
Oven 190°C/375°F. Gas 5.

INGREDIENTS
100g (4 oz) caster sugar
75g (3 oz) ground almonds
25g (1 oz) icing sugar
25g (1 oz) finely flaked blanched
  almonds
2 small egg yolks
finely grated rind of 1 small orange
few drops of almond essence

METHOD
Mix the caster sugar, ground almonds and orange rind together in a medium-sized mixing bowl. Make a well in the centre of the mixture and put in the egg yolks and almond essence. Using a small spatula or your fingers, gradually work in the dry ingredients. Lightly knead the mixture until it forms a smooth paste. Shape it into a ball, wrap it in grease-proof paper and chill it in the fridge for ten minutes.

Sprinkle a board and rolling pin with icing sugar and roll the paste very thinly. Using a 5cm (2 in) pastry cutter, cut the marzipan into circles.

Place them, spaced slightly apart, on a large baking sheet which has been greased with butter. Put a few almonds on each circle.

Bake them in the centre of the

Melting Moments

INGREDIENTS
175g (6 oz) self-raising flour
125g (4 oz) butter
125g (4 oz) caster sugar
1 egg
50g (2 oz) rolled oats
pinch of salt
12 glacé cherries

METHOD
Using a wooden spoon, beat the butter until it is soft and creamy. Beat in the sugar until the mixture is pale and drops easily from the spoon. Beat in the egg with 25g (1 oz) of the flour. Fold in the remaining flour and the salt and mix them to form a stiff dough.

Divide the mixture into 24 pieces and, with wet hands, roll each one into a ball the size of a walnut. Roll the balls in the oats and place them on baking trays, allowing room for them to spread. Flatten each one slightly. Place half a glacé cherry in the centre of each biscuit. Bake them for 20 minutes. Allow them to set a little on the trays before cooling them on a rack. This recipe makes 24 biscuits.
Oven 180°C/350°F. Gas 4.

N

Napoleon Biscuits

rings and rounds together.
Oven 200°C/400°F. Gas 6.

INGREDIENTS
Biscuits:
100g (4 oz) plain flour
60g (2½ oz) margarine
35g (1½ oz) caster sugar
25g (1 oz) cornflour
1 egg yolk

Decoration:
icing sugar
jam

METHOD
Sieve together the flour and cornflour. Rub the fat in finely. Add the sugar and bind the mixture to a soft dough with the egg yolk.

Roll the dough out to a thickness of 0.5cm (¼ in). Cut out an equal number of rounds and circles with their middles removed to make rings. Place them on a greased baking tray. Prick the rounds only. Bake them for 10 to 15 minutes.

When they are cool, spread the rounds with jam. Dust the rings with icing sugar and sandwich the

Napoleon Hats

smooth mixture. When the biscuits are cold, top each one with a little icing.
Oven 180°C/350°F. Gas 4.

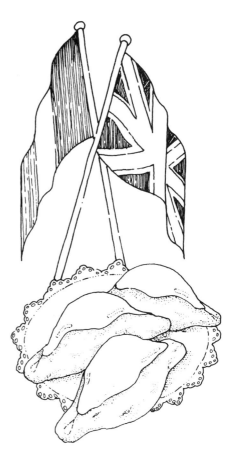

INGREDIENTS
Biscuits:
100g (4 oz) plain flour
50g (2 oz) butter
50g (2 oz) caster sugar
½ egg
pinch of baking powder

Almond paste:
50g (2 oz) icing sugar
25g (1 oz) ground almonds
a little egg

Icing:
50g (2 oz) icing sugar
2 tsp water

METHOD
For the biscuits, cream the butter and sugar. Mix them to a stiff dough with the beaten egg, sifted flour and baking powder. Roll it out thinly and cut it into rounds.

To prepare the almond paste, bind the icing sugar and ground almonds with the beaten egg and mix to a smooth consistency. Roll the almond paste into balls and place one on each biscuit. Fold up the two sides of the biscuits to make a shape like Napoleon's hat. Bake them for approximately 20 minutes in a moderate oven.

For the icing, mix the icing sugar with the water and beat them to a

Novelty Biscuits

INGREDIENTS
100g (4 oz) self-raising flour
50g (2 oz) caster sugar
50g (2 oz) margarine
10g (½ oz) chopped walnuts
10g (½ oz) glacé cherries
2 tsp desiccated coconut
4 tsp beaten egg
pinch of salt

METHOD
Cream the margarine and sugar.
Mix together the dry ingredients
and, gradually add them, together
with the chopped glacé cherries, to
the creamed mixture. Bind the
dough together with the egg. Roll it
out and cut it into shapes. Bake
them for 15 to 20 minutes in a
moderate oven.
Oven 180°C/350°F. Gas 4.

Nut and Fruit Shortbread

INGREDIENTS
225g (8 oz) plain flour
175g (6 oz) butter
75g (3 oz) caster sugar
50g (2 oz) blanched almonds
25g (1 oz) glacé cherries
25g (1 oz) ground rice
25g (1 oz) angelica

METHOD
Cream the butter and sugar. Add
the ground rice and sieved flour.
Stir in the chopped cherries,
angelica and half of the almonds.
   Place the dough in a square-
shaped tin and press the remainder
of the almonds on the top. Bake it
for 30 to 40 minutes.
Oven 180°C/350°F. Gas 4.

O

Oat Biscuits

INGREDIENTS
125g (4 oz) rolled oats
125g (4 oz) plain flour
125g (4 oz) caster sugar
125g (4 oz) butter
1 tbsp golden syrup
1 tsp bicarbonate of soda
1 tbsp water

METHOD
Sift the flour and bicarbonate of soda, and mix all the dry ingredients together. Dissolve the butter, sugar and syrup in the water over a low heat, then stir them into the dry mixture.

Put teaspoonfuls on a very well greased baking sheet leaving room for the biscuits to spread. Bake them on the top shelf of the oven for 15 to 20 minutes. Leave them to cool for only a few seconds, then loosen them with a knife. Cool them on a wire tray.
Oven 180°C/350°F. Gas 4.

Oatmeal Biscuits

INGREDIENTS
175g (6 oz) coarse oatmeal
150g (5 oz) plain flour
125g (4 oz) caster sugar
75g (3 oz) butter
a little milk
1 tsp baking powder

METHOD
Rub the butter into the dry ingredients, then add the milk. Roll out the dough and cut it into shapes. Bake them in a slow oven on well greased trays for about 15 to 20 minutes.
Oven 150°C/300°F. Gas 2.

Orange Coconut Crisps

INGREDIENTS
75g (3 oz) butter or margarine
50g (2 oz) caster sugar
50g (2 oz) plain flour
25g (1 oz) cornflour
pinch of salt
rind of 1 orange
orange juice
desiccated coconut

METHOD
Cream together the fat and sugar
until they are light and fluffy, then
beat in the grated orange rind. Add
the sifted flour, cornflour and salt
and mix them to form a dough.

Shape the dough into about 15
small balls. Brush each one with
orange juice and roll them in the
coconut. Place them on a greased
baking tray and flatten them
slightly. Bake them for 18 minutes
in a moderate oven.
Oven 180°C/350°F. Gas 4.

P

Peanut Butter Cookies

INGREDIENTS
100g (4 oz) self-raising flour
50g (2 oz) caster sugar
50g (2 oz) butter
3 tbsp light brown sugar
3 tsp peanut butter
1 egg
grated rind of ½ orange

METHOD
Cream the peanut butter, orange
rind, butter and both sugars until
the mixture is light and fluffy.
Work in the beaten egg and stir in
the flour to make a firm mixture.
Roll the dough into walnut-sized
pieces and place them, spaced well
apart, on a greased baking tray.
Dip a fork in a little flour and press
criss-cross lines on top of each one.
Bake for 25 minutes until they are
risen and golden brown.
Oven 180°C/350°F. Gas 4.

Peanut Cookies

INGREDIENTS
150g (5 oz) self-raising flour
125g (4 oz) caster sugar
125g (4 oz) soft margarine
50g (2 oz) salted peanuts

METHOD
Cream the margarine and sugar
together thoroughly. Chop the nuts
and stir them into the mixture with
the flour. Place walnut-sized balls
of the dough on a greased tray.
Bake them in a moderate oven for
about 20 minutes.
Oven 180°C/350°F. Gas 4.

Peppermint Oat Biscuits

sieved icing sugar and cream them together. Add the peppermint essence and beat the mixture well.

When the biscuits are cold, sandwich them together with the filling.

Oven 200°C/400°F. Gas 6.

INGREDIENTS
Biscuits:
225g (8 oz) plain flour
225g (8 oz) rolled oats
175g (6 oz) sugar
125g (4 oz) lard
125g (4 oz) margarine
2 tsp golden syrup
1 tsp baking powder
2 tsp vanilla essence
¼ tsp bicarbonate of soda
4 tsp boiling water

Filling:
150g (6 oz) icing sugar
75g (3 oz) butter
few drops peppermint essence

METHOD
To make the biscuits, cream together the lard, margarine, syrup and sugar. Dissolve the bicarbonate of soda in the boiling water and add it to the creamed mixture together with all the other ingredients. Roll out the dough and cut it into rounds. Bake them on well greased trays for 15 to 20 minutes or until they are pale brown.

For the filling, cream the butter until it is soft. Gradually add the

Petits Fours

INGREDIENTS
50g (2 oz) ground almonds
50g (2 oz) caster sugar
1 egg
glacé cherries
angelica
rice paper

METHOD
Beat the egg then mix it to a paste
with the almonds and sugar. Place
the mixture in a forcing bag with a
large star nozzle and pipe small
shapes onto rice paper. Allow them
to stand for 24 hours.

Decorate them with angelica and
cherries and bake them for 15 to 20
minutes or until they are light
brown.
Oven 180°C/350°F. Gas 4.

R

Raisin Shortcake

INGREDIENTS
175g (6 oz) plain flour
125g (4 oz) seedless raisins
125g (4 oz) butter
50g (2 oz) caster sugar
4 tbsp orange juice

METHOD
Put the orange juice and raisins
into a pan and bring them slowly
to the boil. Leave them to cool.
Rub the butter into the flour and
sugar until the mixture resembles
fine breadcrumbs. Knead the
dough well, then divide it into two
equal rounds.
  Put one on a greased baking
sheet and spread it with the raisin
mixture. Top this with the second
round and press them firmly
together. Prick it well and bake it
for 45 minutes. Mark it into
sections. Remove it from the
baking sheet when it is cold.
Oven 180°C/350°F. Gas 4.

Rice Biscuits

INGREDIENTS
225g (8 oz) self-raising flour
175g (6 oz) caster sugar
175g (6 oz) margarine
125g (4 oz) ground rice
4 tbsp milk
¼ tsp lemon essence
glacé cherries

METHOD
Mix together thoroughly the flour,
rice and sugar. Rub in the
margarine. Mix them to a stiff
paste with the milk and lemon
essence.
  Roll the dough out thinly and
cut it into rounds with a scone
cutter. Decorate each one with a
small piece of cherry. Place them
on a greased baking sheet and bake
them in a moderate oven for about
15 minutes.
Oven 180°C/350°F. Gas 4.

Rich Biscuits

INGREDIENTS
225g (8 oz) self-raising flour
125g (4 oz) caster sugar
125g (4 oz) margarine or butter
1 egg
rind and juice of ½ lemon

METHOD
Mix the flour and sugar in a bowl.
Rub in the margarine until the
mixture looks like breadcrumbs.
Add the grated lemon rind. Mix to
a stiff paste with the beaten egg
and lemon juice.

Roll the dough out thinly and
cut it into approximately 40 rounds
with a scone cutter. Place them on
greased baking sheets. Bake them
in a moderate oven for about 15
minutes.
Oven 180°C/350°F. Gas 4.

Rolled Oat Biscuits

INGREDIENTS
225g (8 oz) butter or margarine
175g (6 oz) plain flour
125g (4 oz) moist brown sugar
75g (3 oz) rolled oats
pinch of bicarbonate of soda
pinch of salt

METHOD
Mix all the ingredients together
thoroughly. Roll the dough out on
a floured board, but do not make it
too thin. Cut it into shapes and
place them on greased trays. Cook
them in a slow oven for 20 to 25
minutes until they are brown.
Oven 150°C/300°F. Gas 2.

S

Semolina Pyramid Biscuits

INGREDIENTS
75g (3 oz) butter
50g (2 oz) sugar
50g (2 oz) cornflour
25g (1 oz) semolina
a little jam

METHOD
Cream the butter and sugar. Mix the cornflour and semolina and add them to the creamed mixture. Knead it well.

Roll the dough out thinly. Cut out equal numbers of rounds with a 2.5cm (1 in) fluted cutter, a 4cm (1½ in) plain cutter, and a 5cm (2 in) fluted cutter. Put them on greased trays and bake them for 15 minutes.

When they are cold, sandwich the three rounds together with jam to form pyramid shapes.
Oven 180°C/350°F. Gas 4.

Shortbread Biscuits

INGREDIENTS
150g (6 oz) plain flour
100g (4 oz) butter
50g (2 oz) caster sugar

METHOD
Knead the ingredients together until the mixture has a soft consistency. Roll it out and cut it into fingers. Leave them overnight on a baking sheet. Bake them in a hot oven for 10 to 12 minutes or until they are golden brown.
Oven 200°C/400°F. Gas 6.

Shrewsbury Biscuits

INGREDIENTS
225g (8 oz) plain flour
125g (4 oz) butter
125g (4 oz) sugar
25g (1 oz) currants
1 egg
pinch of bicarbonate of soda
rind and juice of ½ lemon

METHOD
Cream the butter and sugar, then add the egg, lemon rind and juice, currants, flour and bicarbonate of soda. Knead well, and leave the mixture in the fridge overnight.

Roll it out to a thickness of 0.5cm (¼ in) and cut it into rounds. Bake them on greased trays for about 20 minutes.
Oven 180°C/350°F. Gas 4.

Strawberry Delights

INGREDIENTS
225g (8 oz) dates
125g (4 oz) rice crispies
125g (4 oz) granulated sugar
75g (3 oz) chopped nuts
75g (3 oz) desiccated coconut
5 tbsp butter or margarine
2 eggs
1 tsp vanilla essence
pinch of salt
few drops red food colouring

METHOD
Melt the butter in a pan, add the chopped dates and cook them over a low heat. When the mixture begins to thicken, add the beaten eggs, salt and vanilla. Allow the mixture to cool a little, then add the rice crispies, nuts and coconut. Turn the mixture onto a large plate and leave it to go cool.

Take small pieces of the mixture and shape them into "strawberries". Roll them in red sugar which is made by mixing red food colouring into the granulated sugar. Top each one with a leaf of green angelica or marzipan.

This recipe is excellent for freezing.

T

Tebay Crunch

INGREDIENTS
350g (12 oz) rolled oats
225g (8 oz) butter
125g (4 oz) caster sugar

METHOD
Heat the butter and sugar in a pan, add the oats gradually, then mix them well together.

Turn the mixture into a greased dish and brown it in the oven for 15 to 20 minutes. Cut it into pieces when it is cold.
Oven 180°C/350°F. Gas 4.

Tuilles

INGREDIENTS
85g (3½ oz) caster sugar
50g (2 oz) melted butter
35g (1½ oz) plain flour
15g (½ oz) ground almonds
1 egg white
grated rind of ½ lemon or orange

METHOD
Whisk the egg white. Add the sugar, re-whisk, then add the lemon rind. Mix together the flour and ground almonds and fold them into the mixture along with the melted butter. Place half-teaspoonfuls of the mixture on a greased tray, leaving space between each one. Bake for 5 to 6 minutes.

While the tuilles are still warm, lay them over a greased rolling pin to make them curl.

These biscuits are usually served with a rich party dessert.
Oven 190°C/375°F. Gas 5.

V

Vanilla Kipferl

slow oven for 20 minutes or until they are a pale golden colour. Leave them for three minutes to firm up and dip them in a bowl of icing or caster sugar. This recipe makes 48 biscuits.
Oven 160°C/325°F. Gas 3.

INGREDIENTS
225g (8 oz) plain flour
225g (8 oz) butter
125g (4 oz) caster sugar
125g (4 oz) ground almonds or hazelnuts or a mixture of half and half
1 tsp vanilla essence
pinch of salt
sieved icing or caster sugar for coating

METHOD
Work the butter into the flour, salt, essence, nuts and caster sugar until a dough is formed. Chill it for one hour.

Pinch off pieces the size of a walnut and roll them into "pencils" about 2cm (¾ in) thick and 6cm (2½ in) long, then bend them into a crescent. When forming the biscuits, try not to use any flour as this will toughen them.

Arrange them on ungreased trays, leaving about 2.5cm (1 in) between each biscuit, as they do spread. Bake them in a moderately

Viennese Biscuits

INGREDIENTS
100g (4 oz) butter or margarine
100g (4 oz) plain flour
25g (1 oz) icing sugar
vanilla essence
glacé cherries

METHOD
Cream the butter and sugar, stir in
a few drops of essence and
gradually work in the flour.

Put the mixture in a forcing bag
and pipe fingers, rounds, or other
shapes. Decorate them with a cherry.
Bake them for 15 to 20 minutes.
Leave them to cool before removing
them from the tray.
Oven 180°C/350°F. Gas 4.

W

Walnut Bars

INGREDIENTS
225g (8 oz) butter
225g (8 oz) caster sugar
200g (7 oz) plain flour
50g (2 oz) chopped walnuts
1 tsp vanilla essence
1 egg

METHOD
Separate the egg. Cream the butter and sugar. Mix in the egg yolk, vanilla essence and the flour. Press the mixture into a greased oblong tin size 25 x 18 x 5cm (10 x 7 x 2 in).

Lightly whisk the egg white and brush it over the mixture. Sprinkle on the walnuts and bake for 45 minutes.
Oven 180°C/350°F. Gas 4.

Walnut Crisps

INGREDIENTS
225g (8 oz) self-raising flour
225g (8 oz) brown sugar
100g (4 oz) walnuts
100g (4 oz) plain chocolate
75g (3 oz) margarine
1 egg

METHOD
Rub the margarine into the flour and sugar. Break the chocolate into pieces and add them together with the broken walnuts. Bind the mixture with the egg.

Place small heaps of the dough on a greased baking sheet and flatten them with a fork. Bake them for about 15 minutes.
Oven 180°C/350°F. Gas 4.

Wheaten Biscuits

Wholemeal Shortcake

INGREDIENTS
150g (5 oz) rolled oats
125g (4 oz) margarine
50g (2 oz) caster sugar
50g (2 oz) plain wholemeal flour
½ tsp salt
pinch of bicarbonate of soda

METHOD
Cream together the margarine and sugar, then gradually work in the flour, salt and baking powder. Turn the mixture out onto a floured board and sprinkle it with the oats.

Roll the dough out to a thickness of 1cm (½ in) and score it with a fork to roughen the surface. Cut it into shapes and bake for 15 to 20 minutes or until the biscuits are a light golden colour.
Oven 190°C/375°F. Gas 5.

INGREDIENTS
225g (8 oz) wholemeal flour
125g (4 oz) butter
50g (2 oz) barbados sugar
25g (1 oz) ground almonds
½ egg yolk
pinch of salt

METHOD
Cream the butter and sugar until they are soft and creamy. Stir in the dry ingredients then add the egg yolk. Form the dough into rounds or roll it out and cut it into pieces. Bake for about 15 to 20 minutes.
Oven 165°C/325°F. Gas 3.

Y

Yo-Yo's

together with the filling.
Oven 180°C/350°F. Gas 4.

INGREDIENTS
Biscuits:
175g (6 oz) self-raising flour
175g (6 oz) margarine
50g (2 oz) custard powder
50g (2 oz) icing sugar
½ tsp vanilla essence

Filling:
100g (4 oz) icing sugar
50g (2 oz) butter
2-3 drops vanilla essence

METHOD
For the biscuits, cream the
margarine and sugar. Work in the
flour and custard powder. Add the
vanilla.

Roll the dough into balls and
place them on a baking sheet. Mark
them with the back of a fork. Bake
them in a moderate oven for 10
minutes. Cool them on a wire tray.

To make the filling, cream the
butter until it is soft. Gradually
add the sieved icing sugar and
cream them together. Add the
vanilla essence and beat the
mixture well. Sandwich the biscuits

Savoury
Biscuits

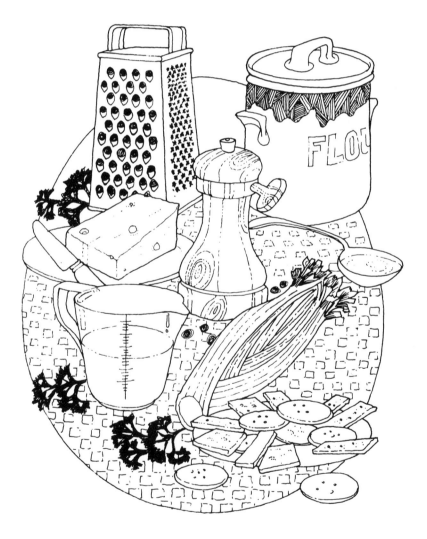

Bacon and Oatmeal Biscuits

INGREDIENTS
125g (4 oz) rolled oats
125g (4 oz) self-raising flour
125g (4 oz) hard margarine
75-100g (3-4 oz) finely minced lean
  bacon
1 small egg
1 tsp dry mustard
salt and pepper

METHOD
Rub the margarine into the oats
and flour. Add the salt and pepper,
mustard and bacon. Mix them
together well before adding the
beaten egg.

Roll the dough out fairly thinly
and cut it into any shape required.
Bake them for 15 minutes or until
they are golden brown. This recipe
makes 30 small biscuits.
Oven 180°C/350°F. Gas 4.

Celery Biscuits

INGREDIENTS
225g (8 oz) plain flour
50g (2 oz) margarine
2 tsp celery seeds
"top of milk" or single cream to
  mix
pinch of salt

METHOD
Rub the fat into the flour. Add the
salt and the seeds. Mix them to a
stiff, pliable dough with the liquid.
Knead it thoroughly, roll it out
thinly and cut it into rounds. Bake
them on a greased tray for 10 to 15
minutes.

Serve them alone, with butter or
cheese or with both.
Oven 200°C/400°F. Gas 6.

Cheese Biscuits

Cheese Crackers

INGREDIENTS
225g (8 oz) plain flour
225g (8 oz) cheese
75g (3 oz) butter
1 tsp baking powder
1 egg yolk
good pinch of salt
pinch of cayenne
cold water

METHOD
Rub the butter into the flour. Add
the salt, baking powder, cayenne
and grated cheese. Beat the egg
yolk with a little cold water and
add it to the rest of the ingredients.
Mix them to a stiff dough.

Knead it a little on a floured
board, roll it out and stamp it into
rounds. Place them on a greased
baking sheet and bake them for 10
to 15 minutes in a hot oven until
they are pale golden brown.
Oven 200°C/400°F. Gas 6.

INGREDIENTS
100g (4 oz) self-raising flour
50g (2 oz) butter or margarine
25g (1 oz) cheese
pinch of salt
cold water

METHOD
Sift the flour and salt into a basin,
then add the finely grated cheese.
Mix them to a firm dough with the
cold water and knead the mixture
until it is smooth.

Roll it into a 23 x 13 cm (9 x 5
in) oblong. Mark it lightly into
three portions. Spread 25g (1 oz) of
the butter over two-thirds of the
dough, and fold the unbuttered
portion between the two buttered
portions, envelope fashion. Give
the dough a half-turn, and roll it
again, a little larger than the
original oblong. Repeat the process
with the remainder of the butter,
and fold it again. Put in cool place
for 30 minutes.

Roll it out and fold it once more
(with no fat), then roll to less than
0.5cm (¼ in) thick. Cut it into
squares. Prick them all over and
bake them for 15 to 20 minutes.
Oven 160°C/325°F. Gas 3.

Cheese Sablés

INGREDIENTS
75g (3 oz) cheese
75g (3 oz) plain flour
75g (3 oz) butter
1 egg
salt and pepper to taste

METHOD
Sift the flour. Cut the butter into pieces and rub it into the flour. Add the grated cheese and season with the salt and pepper. Press the mixture together to make a dough. Wrap the dough in greaseproof paper and chill it in the fridge for about 30 minutes.

Carefully roll out the dough until it is fairly thin. Cut it into strips about 5cm (2 in) wide and brush with the lightly beaten egg. Cut the strips into triangles. Place them on a baking tray lined with greaseproof paper and bake for 10 minutes until the biscuits are golden brown.
Oven 190°C/375°F. Gas 5.

Cheese Straws or Biscuits

INGREDIENTS
75g (3 oz) plain flour
50g (2 oz) margarine or butter
50g (2 oz) cheese
½ tsp salt
pinch of pepper
pinch of cayenne

METHOD
Rub the cheese through a wire sieve. Add the salt, pepper and cayenne to the flour. Partly cream the fat, then add the cheese and the seasoned flour. Mix it to a paste and allow it to stand for at least half an hour.

Roll it out on a lightly floured board and cut it into straws or biscuits. Place them on a baking sheet and prick them. Cook them in a moderate oven for about 15 minutes.
Oven 180°C/350°F. Gas 4.

Crackamacs

INGREDIENTS
100g (4 oz) self-raising flour
½ tsp salt
milk or water to mix

METHOD
Sift the flour and salt into a basin.
Add the milk or water and mix
with a fork to make a dough.
   Roll it out very thinly on a
floured board and cut it into
rounds or squares. Bake in hot
oven for 10 to 15 minutes. Serve
with cheese.
Oven 200°C/400°F. Gas 6.

Curry Knots

INGREDIENTS
100g (4 oz) plain flour
50g (2 oz) margarine
2 tsp curry powder
pinch of salt
egg yolk or water to mix
egg yolk to glaze

METHOD
Rub the fat into the flour. Add the
sieved curry powder and salt; mix
well. Bind the mixture to a stiff but
pliable dough with a little egg yolk
or water.
   Knead the dough well to remove
any cracks and roll it into a long
strip about 2 cm (¾ in) thick. Cut
this into 15cm (6 in) long pieces
and tie each one into a knot. Brush
them with beaten egg yolk and
bake in a moderate oven for about
10 to 15 minutes or until they are
golden. This recipe make approximately 18 biscuits.
Oven 180°C/350°F. Gas 4.

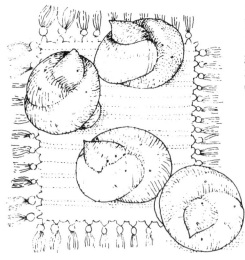

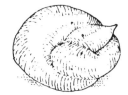

Digestive Biscuits

Guernsey Biscuits

INGREDIENTS
175g (6 oz) wholewheat flour
75g (3 oz) butter or margarine
40g (1½ oz) soft bown sugar
25g (1 oz) oatmeal
2-3 tbsp milk
1 tsp baking powder
½ tsp salt

METHOD
Mix together the flour and oatmeal.
Sift in the salt and baking powder
and rub in the fat. Stir in the
sugar. Add the milk and mix to a
stiff dough.

Roll the dough out thinly and
prick it well. Cut out 6cm (2½ in)
rounds with a plain cutter. Place
them on a baking tray and bake for
15 to 20 minutes. Serve with
cheese.
Oven 190°C/375°F. Gas 5.

INGREDIENTS
450g (1 lb) plain flour
250ml (8 fl oz) warm milk or
   water
125g (4 oz) margarine
25g (1 oz) fresh yeast
15g (½ oz) caster sugar
15g (½ oz) salt

METHOD
Cream together the yeast and
sugar. Add the liquid and leave this
mixture in a warm place until it is
frothy. Sift the flour and salt and
rub in the fat. Add the yeast
mixture to the flour and knead
well. Leave the dough to rise in a
warm place for 1 hour.

Knock back the dough and knead
again. Form it into balls about 2cm
(1 in) in diameter. Flatten the balls
and roll them out. Place them on a
greased baking tray and allow them
to prove for 15 to 20 minutes in a
warm place. Bake for 20 minutes.
This recipe makes approximately
40 biscuits.
Oven 200°C/400°F. Gas 6.

Oatcakes

INGREDIENTS
450g (1 lb) medium oatmeal
225g (8 oz) plain flour
125g (4 oz) margarine
5 tbsp lukewarm water
1 tbsp caster sugar
1 tsp bicarbonate of soda
1 tsp salt

METHOD
Sift the flour, salt and bicarbonate
of soda. Mix in the sugar and
oatmeal and bind with the melted
margarine and water.

Roll the dough out to a thickness
of about 3mm (⅛ in) and cut it out
into 5cm (2 in rounds). Place them
on a greased baking tray and bake
for 20 minutes. These taste very
good when served with cheese.
Oven 190°C/375°F. Gas 5.

Paprika Cheese Biscuits

INGREDIENTS
175g (6 oz) plain flour
175g (6 oz) butter
75g (3 oz) Cheddar cheese
50g (2 oz) almonds with skins on
1 egg yolk
½ tsp paprika
beaten egg to glaze

METHOD
Rub the butter into the flour. Add
the finely grated cheese, paprika
and the lightly beaten egg yolk. Stir
in the nuts and work the mixture
to a smooth dough.

Roll it out to a thickness of 1cm
(½ in). Cut out shapes with a small
plain cutter. Brush the tops with
beaten egg and sprinkle lightly with
a little more cheese or paprika.
Bake for about 20 minutes.
Oven 160°C/325°F. Gas 3.

Walnut Savoury Biscuits

INGREDIENTS
175g (6 oz) plain flour
75g (3 oz) margarine
75g (3 oz) Cheddar cheese
50g (2 oz) rolled oats
50g (2 oz) chopped walnuts
1 egg
½ tsp salt
½ tsp dry mustard
pinch of pepper
150 ml (¼ pt) cold water

METHOD
Sieve together the dry ingredients, add the oats and rub in the margarine. Stir in the grated cheese and walnuts. Beat the egg and reserve a teaspoonful for the glaze. Add the egg to the mixture and bind it to a stiff dough with the water.

Roll out the mixture and trim it to make a rectangle. Add a pinch of salt to the remaining egg and brush this over the surface. Sprinkle the top with a few chopped nuts. Cut it into shapes and bake them for 12 to 15 minutes.
Oven 190°C/375°F. Gas 5.

Wholemeal Savoury Titbits

INGREDIENTS
Biscuits:
100g (4 oz) wholemeal flour
25g (1 oz) lard
½ tsp baking powder
pinch of salt
milk to mix

Topping:
4 tbsp cream cheese
1 tbsp grated cheese
1 tbsp chopped celery
salt, pepper and mustard to taste
parsley and red pepper to garnish

METHOD
For the biscuits, sieve together the flour, baking powder and salt. Rub in the lard, then mix with enough milk to make a stiff dough. Roll this out very thinly. Prick the dough and cut it into small rounds. Bake in a moderate oven for 10 to 15 minutes until the biscuits are brown and firm. When they are cold store them in an airtight tin.

To make the topping, mix all the ingredients, and pile on to the biscuits. Garnish. This makes enough topping for 8 to 12 biscuits.
Oven 180°C/350°F. Gas 4.

What is the WI?

If you have enjoyed this book, the chances are that you would enjoy belonging to the largest women's organisation in the country — the Women's Institutes.

We are friendly, go-ahead, like-minded women, who derive enormous satisfaction from all the movement has to offer. This list is long — you can make new friends, have fun and companionship, visit new places, develop new skills, take part in community services, fight local campaigns, become a WI market producer, and play an active role in an organisation which has a national voice.

The WI is the only women's organisation with its own adult education establishment, Denman College, where you can take a course in anything from car maintenance to paper sculpture, from book binding to yoga, or cordon bleu cookery to fly-fishing.

All you need to do to join is write to us here at the **National Federation of Women's Institutes, 104 New Kings Road, London SW6 4LY,** or telephone 071 371 9300, and we will put you in touch with WIs in your immediate locality. We hope to hear from you.

If you would like to receive a full catalogue and price-list of further publications, please write to WI Books Ltd, at the above address.

Index

Almond
  Balls, 8
  Butter Crisps, 9
  Cocoroons, 9
  see also Flaked Almond Biscuit,
  German Almond Biscuit
Abbey Biscuits, 8
Alphabet Biscuits, 10
Anzac Cookies, 10
Appleby Fairings, 11
Apricot Shortcakes, 11
Auntie Dot's Cookies, 12
Australian Cookies, see Anzac Cookies

Bacon and Oatmeal Biscuits, 87
Basic Drop Cookies, 13
Belgian Sugar Biscuits, 14
Blantyre Biscuits, 14
Bourbon Biscuits, 15
Bran Crisps, see Crisps
Bufton Biscuits, 16
Burnt Butter Biscuits, 17
Butter Cookies, 17
Buttercrunch, 18

Caramel Biscuits, 19
Caraway Biscuits, 20
Cardomom Cookies, 20
Catherine Wheels, 21
Celery Biscuits, 87
Cheese
  Biscuits, 88,89
  Crackers, 88
  Sables, 89
  Straws, 89
  see also Paprika Cheese Biscuits
Cherry and Chocolate Chews, 22
Cherry
  Snowballs, 22
  Whirls, 23
Chestnut Biscuits, 23

Chocolate
  Biscuits, 24
  Cherry Biscuits, 24
  Chip Biscuits, 25
  Nut Biscuits, 25
  Oat Biscuits, 26
  Peppermint Creams, 27
  Stars, 28
  Wafers, see Basic Drop Cookies
  Wagon Wheels, 28
Cinnamon
  Bars, 29
  Wafer, see Basic Drop Cookies
Coconut
  Biscuits, 29
  Butter Biscuits, 30
  and Cherry Slices, 30
  Crisps, 31
  Drops, 31
  Kisses, 32
  see also Almond Cocoroons,
  Orange Coconut Crisps
Coffee
  Kisses, 32
  Walnut Biscuits, 33
Cornish Ginger Fairings, 33
Coupland Biscuits, 34
Crackamacs, 90
Crescent Biscuits, 34
Creston Drops, 35
Crisps, 35
Crunchies, 36
Crunchy Biscuits, 36
Cumberland Snaps, 37
Curly Peters, 37
Curry Knots, 90

Danish Specier Biscuits, 38
Date
  Slices, 38
  Sticks, 39
Digestive Biscuits (savoury), 91
Dream Cookies, 39
Drop Cookies, 13,40

Easter Biscuits, 41
Easter Bunny Biscuits, 42

Fairings, *see* Appleby, Cornish Ginger
Finnish Shortbread, 43
Firelighter Biscuits, 43
Flaked Almond Biscuits, 44
Florentines, 44
Freezer Biscuits, 45
Fruity Brittles, 46
Fruity Snaps, 46

Garibaldi Biscuits, 47
German Almond Biscuits, 48
German Biscuits, 48
Ginger
    Biscuits, 49
    Ruffles, 50
    Snaps, 50
    see also Cornish Ginger Fairings,
    Grantham Ginger Drops, Iced
    Ginger Shortcake
Gingerbread, *see* Grasmere Gingerbread
Gipsy
    Creams, 51
    Crisps, 52
Grantham Ginger Drops, 52
Grasmere Gingerbread, 53
Greek Butter Cookies, *see* Kourabiedes
Ground Rice Cookies, 53
Guernsey Biscuits, 91

Highlanders, 54
Honey Biscuits, 54

Iced Ginger Shortcake, 55
Iced Peppermint Biscuits, 56
Iced Raspberry Biscuits, 57

Joyce's Biscuits, 58
Jumbles, 58

Kelvin Crisps, 59
King Haakon Biscuits, 60

Kipferl, Vanilla, 81
Kourabiedes, 60
Kringles, 61

Lace Biscuits, 62
Lancashire Nuts, 62
Lemon Crescents, 63
Lemon Fudge Biscuits, 64

Macaroons, 65
Ma' Moule, 65
Marzipan Biscuits, 66

Melting Moments, 67
Mocha butter cream, *see* Bufton Biscuits

Napoleon Biscuits, 68
Napoleon Hats, 69
Novelty Biscuits, 70
Nut and Fruit Shortbread, 70

Oat Biscuits, 71, *see also* Peppermint
    Oat Biscuits, Rolled Oat Biscuits,
    Tebay Crunch
Oatcakes, 92
Oatmeal Biscuits, 71, *see also* Bacon and
    Oatmeal Biscuits
Orange Coconut Crisps, 72

Paprika Cheese Biscuits, 92
Peanut Butter Cookies, 73
Peanut Biscuits, 73
Peppermint Creams, *see* Chocolate
    Peppermint Creams
Peppermint Oat Biscuits, 74
Petit Fours, 75

Raisin Shortcake, 76
Raspberry, *see* Iced Raspberry Biscuits
Rice Biscuits, 76, *see also* Ground Rice
    Cookies
Rolled Oat Biscuits, 77

Semolina Pyramid Biscuits, 78
Shortbread Biscuits, 78, *see also* Finnish
    Shortbread, Nut and Fruit Shortbread
Shrewsbury Biscuits, 79
Shortcake, *see* Apricot, Iced Ginger
    Raisin, Wholemeal Shortcake
Specier Biscuits, *see* Danish Specier Biscuits
Strawberry Delights, 79

Tebay Crunch, 80
Tuilles, 80

Vanilla Kipferl, 81
Viennese Biscuits, 82

Wafer Biscuits, *see* Basic Drop Cookies
Wagon Wheels, *see* Chocolate Wagon Wheels
Walnut
    Bars, 83
    Crisps, 83
    Savoury Biscuits, 93
    see also Coffee Walnut Biscuits
Wheaten Biscuits, 84
Wholemeal
    Savoury Titbits, 93
    Shortcake, 84

Yo-Yo's, 85